The How-To Book of
Interior Walls

No. 898
$8.95

The How–To Book of
Interior Walls
By Don Geary

TAB BOOKS

BLUE RIDGE SUMMIT, PA. 17214

FIRST EDITION

FIRST PRINTING—JULY 1978

Copyright © 1978 by TAB BOOKS

Printed in the United States
of America

Library of Congress Cataloging in Publication Data

Geary, Don.
    The how-to book of interior walls.

    "TAB #898."
    Includes index.
    1. Interior walls—Amateurs' manuals. I. Title.
TH2239.G43   643'.7   77-27860
ISBN 0-8306-8898-6
ISBN 0-8306-7898-0 pbk.

Cover photos by the makers of Armstrong interior furnishings.

Preface

Transform an interior wall and you've transformed a room, changed its character, altered its mood. Wall transformations. That's what this book is all about: vitalizing interior walls in a hundred imaginative, delightful ways—with wallpaper, with paneling, with textured finishes, with brick and stone, with wall graphics, with room dividers, with shingles, with dressed lumber, with windows, with virtually anything that strikes your fancy! This volume teaches you—with step-by-step instructions and detailed illustrations—how to create the effect you want, on any kind of wall surface. There are complete tools and materials lists, precise directions on how to plan each project, plenty of information on wall maintenance, even a section on wall remodeling.

This is a beginner's course that leads you on to advanced know-how, techniques used by professional painters, carpenters, stonemasons, paperhangers, and other craftsmen. And that means do-it-yourself capability, the kind that saves you money—and gives you a world of personal enjoyment.

Don Geary

Other TAB books by the author:

No. 998   *The How-To Book of Floors and Ceilings*

Contents

Chapter 1
Wall
Framing &
Remodeling

Building house walls is really very easy, and fleshing them out with
your favorite wall covering is even simpler. This chapter will show
you *why* it's so easy—and will help you get your bearings in the
pragmatic world of wall remodeling.

WALL FRAMING

The most common wall framing is known as *platform framing*.
After the floor is laid, the walls are built on top of this "platform" and
are raised into place.

The frame of a wall is like a skeleton. In platform framing,
dimensional lumber (commonly 2 × 4 studs) is nailed to sole plates
attached to a subfloor; the studs are capped by top plates (Fig. 1-1).
Each wall frame is fastened to adjoining wall frames with nails and
additional top plates.

The 2 × 4 studs are usually spaced 16 inches apart, or 16
inches O.C. O.C. means on-center: The center of one stud should
be exactly 16 inches from the center of the next. Sometimes,
however, studs are spaced 24 inches O.C. The 24-inch spacing is
not uncommon in single-story houses or for nonload bearing walls.

Studs are spaced at 16- or 24-inch intervals for good reason.
Wallboard, paneling, and plywood come in 4- by 8-foot sheets. If
studs are spaced at 16- or 24-inch intervals, there will always be a
stud to nail the wall covering to.

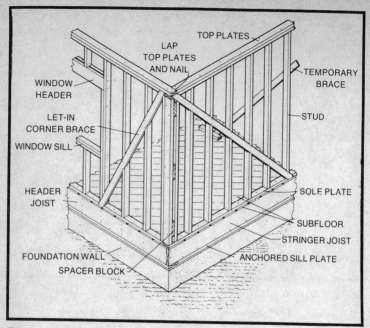

Fig. 1-1. Wall framing platform construction.

To build a wall frame, first lay some 2 × 4s end to end around the perimeter of the house; these 2 × 4s will be the base of the wall, or the sole plates (Fig. 1-1). Turn each sole plate on edge and lay a matching 2 × 4 next to it. The matching 2 × 4s will later become the top of the wall, or the top plates. Mark the pairs of plates for stud placement. Indicate the position of special-purpose studs, such as those that form parts of window frames and those that support window sills.

Incidentally, spaces over windows and doors are filled with larger pieces of lumber called *headers* (Fig. 1-1). Headers usually consist of two 2-inch-thick boards that sandwich a filler (usually 1/4- or 3/4-inch plywood). The following sizes of 2-inch-thick dimensional lumber are used for headers:

MAXIMUM SPAN (feet)	HEADER SIZE (inches)
3 1/2	2 × 6
5	2 × 8
6 1/2	2 × 10
8	2 × 12

The purpose of headers is to help evenly distribute the load of the wall over the span of the door or window opening. Inside the openings, the headers rest on 2 × 4s called *jack studs*. Studs under window openings and upon which the window sill rests are called *cripple studs*.

After the sole and top plates have been marked for stud placement, which is commonly 16 inches O.C., the studs are cut. To insure accuracy, cut all the studs, cripples, and jacks before you start nailing. Cut one stud to the proper length (usually 8 feet), double check your measurement, then mark this stud "pattern stud." All other regular studs can then be cut from this pattern stud, thus insuring uniform stud lengths.

When all the studs, cripples, and jacks have been cut, they can be attached to the sole and top plates. But build the frame for one wall at a time. First nail full-length studs to the plates. Use two sixteenpenny nails to attach each stud end to the plates, nailing through the plates and into the ends of the studs. Next, nail the jacks and cripples to the plates at the appropriate spots. Finally nail the headers. When all the studs have been nailed onto the plates, check the wall frame for squareness. This can be accomplished by measuring diagonally from corner to corner. If the wall frame is square, the two diagonal measurements will be equal.

Now the wall frame must be raised into place and secured to the floor with sixteenpenny nails. It will be helpful to have someone help you tilt the frame into place. It might also be necessary to nail a temporary brace to the frame to help hold it in position while you check for squareness (Fig. 1-1). Before the frame is nailed to the floor it should be plumb. That is, the vertical members (studs) must be at right angles to the floor, and the edge of the sole plate must be flush with the edge of the floor or platform. When the wall frame is plumb, nail the sole plate to the floor. Drive the nails through the sole plate, through the flooring, and into the flooring joists below.

Framing crews that specialize in quick house construction build frames in the above manner and then attach exterior sheathing to the frame *before* tilting it into position. Once the frames have been nailed to the floor, the exterior is practically finished. This is a super quick way to frame and cover exterior walls, but it requires skill and know-how that can only come with a good deal of experience.

After all the exterior (perimeter, or load-bearing) walls have been assembled, raised into position, and nailed to the floor, the

11

interior or nonload-bearing walls can be built. Interior walls should be well fastened to all exterior walls they intersect. This intersection will provide nailing surfaces for plaster-base or gypsum wallboard. This may be accomplished by doubling the exterior wall studs at the intersection. Nailing surfaces for interior wall coverings must be provided at all interior corners.

Interior walls in a house with conventional joist-and-rafter roof construction often serve as load-bearing walls. Such walls help support the weight of joists and beams. Interior walls located parallel to the joists are usually non-load bearing. Studs are 2 × 4s for load-bearing walls but can be 2 × 3s for nonload-bearing walls, However, most contractors use 2 × 4s throughout the house. Spacing of studs is usually controlled by the thickness of the wall covering material. For example, 24-inch stud spacing will require 1/2-inch gypsum board.

An interior wall frame is assembled and erected in the same manner as an exterior wall frame, with a single sole plate and double top plates. The upper top plates are used to tie intersecting wall frames to each other. A single framing stud can be used at each side of a door opening in nonload-bearing walls. However, they must be doubled for load-bearing interior partitions. When roof trusses are used, only the walls that hold up the rafters are load bearing; thus, location of the walls and size and spacing of the studs is determined by room size and interior wall covering. The bottom chords of the trusses are used to fasten and anchor crossing partitions. When partition (interior nonload-bearing) walls are parallel to and located between trusses, they are fastened to 2 × 4 blocks which are nailed between the lower chords.

After all the wall frames are erected (exterior and interior), the upper top plates should be nailed into place to tie all the frames together. These additional top plates add strength and help to unify the whole framing structure (Fig. 1-1). Top plates can also be partly fastened into place when the frames are in horizontal position. Top plates are nailed together with sixteenpenny nails spaced 16 inches apart, with two nails at each intersection. Walls are normally plumbed and aligned *before* the top plate is firmly nailed in place.

By using a 1- by 6-inch or 1- by 8-inch temporary brace on each wall frame, a straight wall is assured (Fig. 1-1). These braces are nailed to the framing studs near the top of the wall; the other ends of the braces are nailed to 2 × 4 "shoe" blocks attached to the sub-floor. The temporary bracing is left in place until the ceiling and roof framing are completed. After the exterior siding or sheeting is attached, the temporary bracing is removed.

WALL REMODELING

If you decide to do some remodeling to an existing wall in your home, first determine what type of wall you will be working on: load-bearing or nonload-bearing. Walls located at right angles to ceiling joists are usually load-bearing walls. Extreme caution should be exercised when doing any work on these walls because of the amount of weight that is supported by them.

Nonload-bearing walls are *usually* located parallel to ceiling joists, but don't be fooled by the direction of the walls. Sometimes interior walls support loads too. Often the floor joists for the room above will sit on top of these walls.

In any event, opening up an existing wall is a dusty, noisy job, so plan on having your household in disorder while remodeling. Begin by removing baseboard and ceiling moldings. If the moldings are pieces of craftsmanship, be careful when you remove them. They may be irreplaceable.

Next, remove the wall covering. Unless your walls are covered with wooden planks or some type of plywood paneling, you won't be able to salvage the wall covering. Plaster or gypsum wallboard does not come off easily, and chances are that you will end up with a pile of dust and small pieces. After you have removed the wall covering the studs are visible, clean up the area. Pick up all the discarded wall covering and get it out of the way; then vacuum the room. This will help prevent dust and pieces of plaster from being tracked all over your house.

An interior wall opening is usually for the addition of a doorway, which means you will have to remove at least two studs and probably relocate two others. A wrecking bar with a claw will come in handy when removing these studs. Chances are that you will be able to salvage them. It makes very good sense to remove the nails from each piece of lumber as it is taken out of the wall.

You may have to relocate electrical wires or plumbing pipes, a job that is best left to an electrician or plumber. Usually if you plan right, you will not have to concern yourself with wiring or plumbing.

If you are opening up an interior wall to the outside, say for a window, there is a trick that can save you some time and needless work. After you have removed the interior wall covering and enough studs to give you the rough opening you will need, mark the opening on the back of the exterior sheeting (from the inside). Drill a hole in the four corners with a hand drill. Then, from the outside, connect the four holes with a pencil and straightedge. Cut out the opening with a hand-held circular saw, using the plunge cut method.

To make a plunge cut, rest the saw on its forward edge and press the rotating blade slowly into the wood along your mark; follow your line until you reach the corner. Repeat the plunge cut until all four sides have been cut; then pop out the cut panel from the inside. Needless to say, extreme caution should be exercised when making this type of cut because the saw will have a tendency to run over the surface rather than cut down into the wood. Your power saw should have two handles; grip both tightly to keep the saw under control.

You must install some type of header over all openings. Doorways will have to have some type of threshold, or sill, to cover the space left in the floor by the opening. If you decide you don't want a threshold, you may have a tough time covering the gap in the floor. If your wood finish flooring runs parallel to the wall that you have opened, the task of filling the gap will be simplified. Simply cut new flooring boards to fit and nail them down. But if you're not so lucky, you'll have to fill the gap with matching flooring and hope for the best. But it is extremely difficult to match older types of floor covering.

A lot of home remodeling requires the building of an interior wall. If you plan carefully, taking into consideration how a new wall will influence air circulation and lighting, the job should go quickly. New interior walls usually don't bear loads, so you have a choice of lumber (2 × 4s or 2 × 3s) and a choice of spacing (16 inches O.C. or 24 inches O.C.). Sixteen-inch spacing is standard for most house construction and will result in a wall of greater strength; 24-inch spacing is not as strong but is good enough for most nonload-bearing walls. It is not uncommon, where building codes permit, to build single-story dwellings with spacing throughout at 24 inches O.C.

Begin by removing any molding or baseboard from the existing wall where the new wall will join it. Next, make marks on the ceiling where the top plate will be fastened. It is imperative that the top plate be nailed to the joists. If the new wall will run parallel to the overhead joists, make sure you nail the plate onto a joist. Obviously, it will be necessary to know where the ceiling joists are before beginning. To find the joists, tap along the ceiling with a hammer, remembering that conventional spacing is 16 inches O.C. Once you find a joist, mark it and the direction it runs.

If the new wall runs between parallel joists, you will have to cut into the ceiling (usually gypsum board) and rig up some type of bracing to help support the top of the new wall. If you do open up the ceiling, you may be getting into a lot more work than you planned for. So if it is at all possible, try to position the new wall so the top plate can be nailed directly into an existing joist.

Nail the top plate to the ceiling. Then drop a plumb line from this plate to the floor and mark the location of the sole plate. Using a plumb line will insure that the two plates will be exactly parallel. Using a ruler to help determine the location of the sole plate can be unreliable. After you have marked the position of the sole plate, nail it in place. Use 3 1/2-inch nails, spaced about 16 inches apart.

After the sole and top plates have been securely fastened, mark the location of the studs on both plates. Remember that spacing is 16 or 24 inches O.C. Cut the required number of studs and toenail them into place. (There should be a stud at each end of the wall, regardless of the spacing.) Start the nails on the ends of the studs, set the studs onto the sole plate, then finish nailing. After you've nailed the studs to the sole plate, check the plumb of the studs and nail them to the top plate. Check the plumb of each stud after it has been nailed to the plates and make sure it is true before moving onto the next stud. If a stud is a little out, you can usually set it plumb by tapping it with a hammer. Drive every nail just below the stud surface. This will save you time and help eliminate problems when you are covering the wall with either gypsum board or paneling.

TOOLS

There are a few tools that are necessary in wall construction and a few tools that will make the work go easier.

Obviously you will need a *hammer*. I've found that a 16-ounce straight claw (ripping) hammer works best for most types of woodworking.

Two rulers will come in handy: a *steel tape ruler* about 20 feet long and an 8-foot *folding ruler*. There are many types of folding rulers, and I have found that the best all-around type is the Lufkin extension rule. On one end of this ruler there is a 6-inch piece of brass that can be extended for inside measurements. When you buy an extension ruler, make sure you oil the joints as soon as you get it; it should last for years.

A 50-foot *chalkline* will prove its worth over and over again on many home remodeling projects. Besides enabling you to mark off long straight lines, a chalkline can be used as a plumb bob.

A good *level* will help you align studs and let you know if the existing walls in your house are straight. Levels come in many different sizes and lengths, but I have found that a 3-foot length is the most useful because it will fit into most areas. I prefer wooden levels over aluminum or plastic, but they all hold up about the same. With a minimum amount of care, a good level should last a lifetime.

A hand held *circulur saw* is not necessary for home remodeling. After all, houses were built before electric saws were invented. But if you have a good circular saw, you will be able to work quickly and more efficiently. For most types of work, a 7 1/4-inch circular saw will be fine. A 2-horsepower motor will give you enough power to cut large-sized lumber. The saw should have two handles, one with a trigger and one to help you guide the saw through cuts. The saw should have a blade guard that slides out of the way as you make a cut and slides back over the blade after the cut is completed. Hand-held circular saws should be double insulated to help protect you from electrical shock. A ripping guide is a handy attachment for these saws; it will enable you to rip lumber to required widths.

I use three kinds of blades with my circular saw: plywood, cross-cut, and 20-tooth carbide-tipped. The plywood blade is used for cutting paneling and other laminated woods. This many-toothed blade cuts clean, with a minimum of splintering. I use my cross-cut blade for cutting across the grain on boards up to 1 inch thick. The carbide-tipped blade probably gets the most use on cutting dimensional lumber (2 × 4s, 2 × 8s, etc.). Some manufacturers claim that a carbide-tipped blade will last about 10 times longer than a regular blade; their claim is close to the mark.

A variable-speed *electric drill* will come in handy for many home improvement projects. I like a drill that is lightweight, powerful, double insulated, and rugged. Drill bits are just as important as the drill itself; if they are dull, they won't do the job and will put excessive strain on the drill motor. Drill bits will keep their sharpness, providing they are not forced to do a job too quickly. Never put all your might behind the drill; this puts undue strain on both the motor and the bit.

A 5-gallon *shop vacuum* will help you clean up during and after your remodeling job. A shop vacuum differs from a home vacuum cleaner in that it can pick up chunks of wood and nails. Some shop vacuums will also suck up liquids.

A wrecking or *pry bar* is useful for tearing down walls, pulling nails, and persuading uncooperative studs and plates. An indispensable tool for all types of interior wall work.

Chapter 2
Gypsum Board

Gypsum panels (or gypsum board) probably cover more interior walls in America than any other type of wall covering material. In fact, gypsum panels are commonly used as backing for finished paneling, tile, and plastic laminate paneling. Gypsum wall panels are relatively inexpensive, can be installed quickly, and provide a strong durable surface for paint, wall paper, and other finish wall coverings. These panels also act as effective noise barriers and are incombustible, so they can be used throughout the home.

THE FACTS ABOUT GYPSUM BOARD

Gypsum board, sometimes called dry wall or Sheetrock (Sheetrock is a registered trademark of United States Gypsum), is made from calcined gypsum mixed with water and other ingredients; the mixture is pressed into a dense panel sandwiched between two sheets of paper. The back side is covered with a strong liner paper; the face side is covered with a heavy manila finished paper.

Gypsum panels are available in thicknesses of 1/4, 3/8, 1/2, and 5/8 inches and in even lengths of 6 to 14 feet. The standard width is 4 feet. The best size for a homeowner to work with is the standard 4-by 8-foot sheet, 1/2 inch thick. The weight of this standard panel is around 2 pounds per square foot, about 60 pounds per sheet. So it will take a bit of muscle to "throw up" these panels, especially overhead.

Gypsum panels have other coverings too. Some panels are covered with foil backing, which acts as an effective vapor barrier. Some are available with a vinyl face; such sheets are stronger than standard paper-covered panels. Although all gypsum panels are fireproof, some are available with superior fire ratings. Such superior fire proof panels are usually limited to thicknesses of 1/2 and 5/8 inch. You can even buy water-resistant gypsum panels for use in high-moisture areas such as the bathroom. Tile or plastic laminated paneling is attached to these water-resistant sheets and helps to prevent moisture from accumulating inside the walls.

In new construction, gypsum panels are often attached directly to wall studs. Problem walls can also be covered, providing the surface of the existing wall is flat and sound. In many instances, a problem wall must first be framed with 2 × 4s or furring strips (1- × 2-inch lumber).

MATERIALS AND TOOLS

The first task in finishing an interior wall with gypsum board is to determine the number of panels (4 by 8 feet) you'll need. Tables 2-1 and 2-2 will aid you in estimating your panel needs.

If you are attaching standard gypsum panels (1/2 inch thick) directly to studs, use annular-ring nails 1 3/8 inch long. The same nails can be used on panels attached directly to furring strips. If, however, you are attaching panels to an existing wall, you should use 2 1/4-inch annular-ring nails. Of course, you'll also need lots of joint compound and tape. See Table 2-3.

If you're not going to use new panels immediately, store them in a dry place. For prolonged storage, the panels should be laid flat. But

Table 2-1. Gypsum Panel Estimating Table.

AREA (IN SQUARE FEET) OF WALLS
PLUS CEILING (OF ROOMS WITH 8-FOOT CEILINGS)

LENGTH OF ROOM (in feet)	WIDTH OF ROOM (in feet)						
	6'	8'	10'	12'	14'	16'	18'
8'	272	320	368	416	464	512	560
10'	316	368	420	472	524	576	628
12'	360	416	472	528	584	640	696
14'	404	464	524	584	644	704	764
16'	448	512	576	640	704	768	832
18'	492	560	628	696	764	832	900
20'	536	608	680	752	824	896	968

Table 2-2. Square Foot Coverage of 4- by 8-Foot Gypsum Panels.

Number of Panels	Coverage (Square Feet)
1	32
5	160
10	320
12	384
14	448
16	512
18	576
20	640
22	704
24	768
26	832
28	896
30	960

if you plan to install them within a short time, say two days, they can be set horizontally on edge. Keep them as straight as possible to prevent warping.

You will not need many tools to cover a wall with gypsum panels. The tools you will need are:

Hammer—16 ounce with a bell-shaped head
Utility knife and extra blades—for cutting the panels
Ruler or straightedge—for measuring and marking panels
Surform tool—for smoothing cut edges of panels
Wall scrapers—for applying joint compound to edges of panels and nail holes (4 to 5 inches wide)
Step ladder
Pencil
Screwdriver
Keyhold saw
Sandpaper

If you have to frame the wall with 2 × 4s or furring strips, you will need a saw for cutting the lumber.

INSTALLATION

No surface preparation is required when gypsum panels are attached directly to studs. Simply nail the panels up, beginning at the ceiling. Panels may be installed vertically (Fig. 2-1A) or horizontally (Fig. 2-1B).

If you are applying gypsum panels over a problem wall (e.g., falling plaster), it is usually best to reframe the wall first with furring strips. Begin by removing all moldings. Knock out loose plaster that sticks out and fill in recesses. You want a wall that is reasonably flat and sound to which you can nail the furring strips.

You can then begin attaching the furring strips to the wall. Nail them flat, from floor to ceiling, with 16-inch spacing between the strips (Fig. 2-2). Nail horizontal pieces of furring *between* the vertical strips at the floor, at the ceiling, and midway between ceiling and floor. The furring strips will provide a sound nailing surface for the gypsum panels. After you cover the wall with the furring strips, you can attach the gypsum panels.

The horizontal method of installation is best for rooms in which a lot of full-length panels can be used. This minimizes the number of vertical joints. For horizontal application, install the top sheets first. Push the boards up firmly against the ceiling and nail. Begin nailing in the center of the boards and space the nails approximately 7 inches

Table 2-3. Estimating Guide Nails, Joint Compound, and Tape.

ESTIMATING GUIDE
NAILS, JOINT COMPOUNT, AND TAPE

Area Covered By Panels (Square feet)	Nails (pounds)	Joint Compound (gallons)	Tape (feet)
100	.6	1	37
200	1.1	2	74
300	1.6	2	111
400	2.1	3	148
500	2.7	3	185
600	3.2	4	222
700	3.7	5	259
800	4.2	5	296
900	4.8	6	333
1000	5.3	7	370

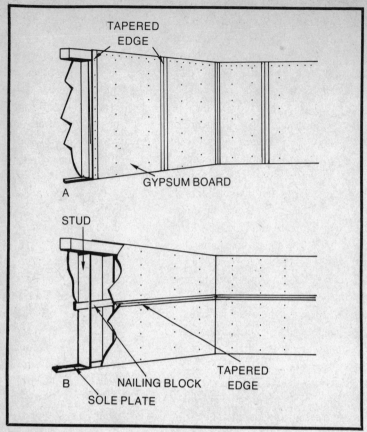

Fig. 2-1. Application of gypsum board finish: A, vertical application; B, horizontal application.

apart. Nail through the panels and into the furring strips below, working from the panel centers towards the edges to prevent bulging. After you install all the top panels horizontally, you can begin nailing the lower panels.

Vertical installation is much the same. Nailing is done from the center of the panels outward; nails are spaced 7 inches apart.

In the application of gypsum panels, the edge of each panel should lie along the center of a framing member—a stud, a furring strip, a sole or top plate, or a nailing block. This will enable you to nail each panel directly to a solid surface.

Joints between panels should be butted closely together. Panels should also fit tightly against the ceiling, unless you plan to attach ceiling molding. Installed panels need not touch the floor; in fact, you can allow a space of up to 2 inches between the floor and the bottom of the panel. This space can be covered with floor molding.

After each nail is driven flush with the face of a panel, tap the nail below surface so that a slight panel dimple is left around each nailhead. Later these dimples can be filled with joint compound. Do not, however, overdrive nailheads or use a nail punch because this will break the face paper. Nails are driven just below the surface of each panel so they won't show when later covered with Spackle. This may seem like a lot of unnecessary work, but if the nailheads are left exposed, they're apt to pop free later. Another reason for spackling nails is that this prevents the nails from rusting. If you are planning to cover the gypsum panels with prefinished paneling, tile, or plastic laminate paneling, spackling of the nailheads will be necessary, but leave dimple marks in all cases.

When you reach the end of a wall, you may have to cut a panel for good fit. Begin by measuring carefully. Mark the panel to be cut with a pencil and straightedge. Then doublecheck your measurements. Then cut the panel with your utility knife. Hold the knife at a right angle to the panel and score the face paper along your mark. For long cuts, use a straightedge or a straight 2 × 4 as a cutting guide. Score the panel while it lies flat on the floor. After the face has been scored about halfway through (this may take a few passes with the knife), pick up the panel and fold it backward, breaking the core of the board along your cut. Then use the knife to cut the back paper. The edges of the cut panel should then be smoothed with a Surform

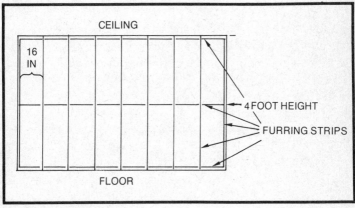

Fig. 2-2. Furring strip placement.

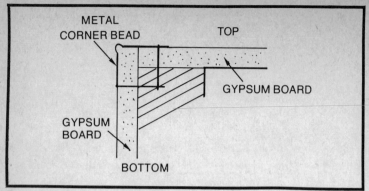

METAL
CORNER BEAD   TOP

                                    GYPSUM BOARD

GYPSUM
BOARD

                    BOTTOM

Fig. 2-3. Attach metal corner beads with nails.

tool. It is important that all edges of cut panels be kept as square as
possible. If you don't have a Surform tool, you can smooth the edges
with a knife.

More than likely you will have to make a hole in a panel for an
electrical outlet, heating register, or some other wall fixture. Measure the exact size and location of the hole and transfer the measurements to the face of the panel. Draw in the hole on the panel.
Next, with a nail or awl, punch several holes through the panel on the
perimeter at the hole. Then with the knife, score the panel along
your marks. Turn the panel over and repeat this process. When both
sides of the panel have been scored, knock out the hole with a
hammer. Remember, you don't have to make an exact cut, but you
should be close. All electrical outlets have strike plates that will
cover holes that are a bit oversized.

Outside corners are especially vulnerable to damage. So to
protect them, you must install metal corner beads (Fig. 2-3). Cut a
strip of corner bead to the proper length and nail it onto the corner, a
nail every 5 inches. Drive the nails through the gypsum board into
the wood framing. Later, you can cover the corner bead with joint
compound.

After the entire wall (or room) has been covered with gypsum
panels, you can begin spackling. Spackle, or joint cement, is available
in powder or premixed form. I prefer the premixed type because it is
much easier to work with and requires no mixing. The powder
variety, however, is less expensive than the premix. *Spackle*, incidentally, is a registered trademark of The Muralo Company, but is
frequently used to describe all kinds of joint compound.

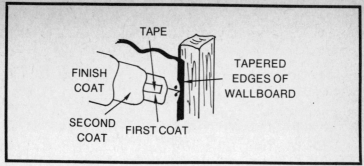

Fig. 2-4. Applying joint compound to joints. (Courtesy Georgia-Pacific)

The purpose of spackling (filling joints between panels and covering nail holes) is to make the finished surface as flat and smooth as possible. After a few tries, you should be able to obtain professional looking results.

Joints *between* panels require the most work, so begin your spackling job with them. Plan on about three days for the job to be completed because each layer of Spackle must dry thoroughly before the next coat is applied (Fig. 2-4).

Using a 4- or 5-inch-wide putty knife, spread the joint compound into the recess formed by the adjoining edges of the panels (Fig. 2-5). While this first coat is still wet, apply perforated wallboard tape over the joint. Center the tape over the joint and press it firmly into the compound with the putty knife until the compound underneath is forced through the openings in the tape (Fig. 2-6). Apply enough pressure to make the tape lie flat on the surface of the wall, but make sure there is enough compound under the tape to insure a good bond. Cover the tape with additional compound and feather (blend) the compound level with the board surface (Fig. 2-7). After

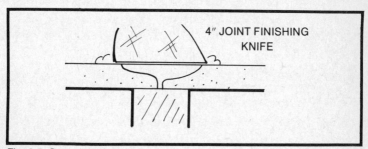

Fig. 2-5. Spread the joint compound evenly into the joint and its surrounding recess. (Courtesy Georgia-Pacific)

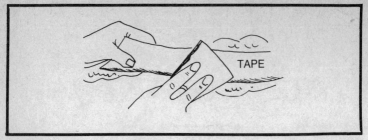

Fig. 2-6. Embed the wallboard tape in the compound. (Courtesy Georgia-Pacific)

this first coat has thoroughly dried (at least 24 hours), sand it lightly and apply the second coat of compound. Again feather the edges of the compound. Let dry and sand. For best results, apply a third coat too. This coat should be 12 to 14 inches wide, applied with a wide-blade putty knife or joint finishing knife. The third coat is the finish coat, so when you are done, there should be no visible lines or seams. If necessary, you can sand lightly after the finish coat has dried. But sand carefully (Fig. 2-8).

Inside corners are treated in a similar fashion. Spread a coat of joint compound into the corner (Fig. 2-9). Cut a length of tape (2 inches wide) and fold it down the center to a right angle (Fig. 2-10). Press the folded tape into the corner forcing the excess joint compound through the holes in the tape. Apply another light coat of the compound to the face of the tape and feather the edges. After this coat dries, sand it smooth and apply a second coat, feathering the edges.

Outside corners, after they have been covered with corner bead, usually require the most work. Tape is not necessary for

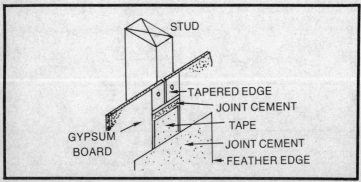

Fig. 2-7. Feather the edge of the joint compound.

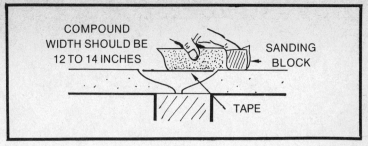

COMPOUND WIDTH SHOULD BE 12 TO 14 INCHES

SANDING BLOCK

TAPE

Fig. 2-8. Sand down the finish coat after it has dried. (Georgia-Pacific)

outside corners covered with corner beads. Begin with a 5-inch putty knife. Lay enough compound onto one side of the corner bead to cover about 2 feet of the bead at a time (Fig. 2-11). To level the compound, let one side of the knife edge ride on the nose of the bead while the other side rides on the gypsum panel (Fig. 2-11). Completely fill the flange of the bead with the compound; feather the compound out to at least 4 inches from the bead edge. Repeat, filling the flange on the other side of the corner. Allow this first coat of compound to dry completely, then sand lightly and apply a second coat of joint compound, carefully feathering the edges. After the second coat has dried, apply the third and final coat. If necessary, the corner can be lightly sanded after the third coat has dried.

Nailheads and accompanying dimples must also be filled with joint compound. First, draw the bare putty knife over each nailhead. If you hear a metallic ring, drive the nailhead below the surface with

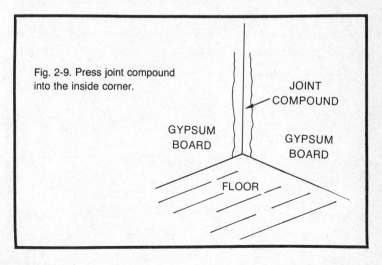

Fig. 2-9. Press joint compound into the inside corner.

JOINT COMPOUND

GYPSUM BOARD

GYPSUM BOARD

FLOOR

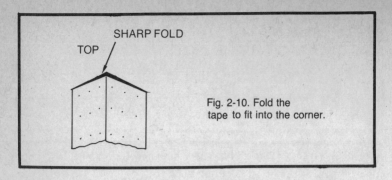

SHARP FOLD

TOP

Fig. 2-10. Fold the
tape to fit into the corner.

your hammer. Working on one nail at a time, fill the dimples with compound. Apply the compound with a sweep of the knife in one direction (Fig. 2-12). Wipe off excess compound with a sweep of the knife in the opposite direction, smoothing the compound level with the surface. After the first coat of compound has dried, apply a second and final coat in the same manner. Let dry; sand lightly if necessary.

After you have completed all spackling (and surfaces have dried), look over the job. Apply an additional coat of compound to any areas that are not perfect. You are finished when the walls look solid, flat, and smooth. Then you're ready to apply the finish covering of your choice—paint, wallpaper, etc.

Some more tips on joint treatment and spackling are in order here. Never apply Spackle over partially dried areas. This will result in uneven drying; cracks will surely appear later. Joint compound should not be applied if the room temperature is below 50 degrees. Protect premixed compound from extreme heat and freezing by storing in a tightly sealed container. The unused portion will last for several years. Spackling and taping is not necessary if the wall will be

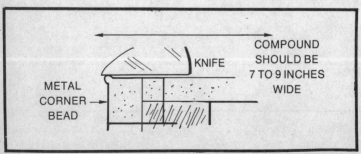

COMPOUND
SHOULD BE
7 TO 9 INCHES
WIDE

KNIFE

METAL
CORNER
BEAD

Fig. 2-11. Finishing the metal corner bead. (Courtesy Georgia-Pacific)

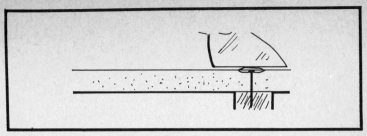

Fig. 2-12. Finishing nailheads. (Courtesy Georgia-Pacific)

covered with a solid wall covering such as tile, prefinished wood paneling, or plastic laminate. Sanding of hardened joint compound is an extremely dusty process, so protect your home by keeping the room you are working in closed off to the rest of the house. Vacuum after sanding to prevent Spackle dust from being tracked all over your house. If you are planning to finish your remodeling job with a fresh coat of paint, you must first apply a primer to all spackled areas.

Chapter 3
Painting Your Walls

Painting is often the quickest and least expensive way to change the appearance of your walls. Some walls will have problems which must be corrected before painting, but the basic work pattern should follow these steps: planning, surface preparation, then painting.

COLOR

The first decision that must be made in painting a wall is, of course, the color. Interior decorators use color to effectively change the character of a room. Probably the most ineffectual paint is basic white; it says nothing. Of course, there are times when you don't want your walls to say anything: when works of art are hung or when a window with a view is present.

Here are a few guidelines that may be helpful to you in deciding which color(s) to use in a room:

1. Light colors will make a room look larger. Conversely, darker colors will make a room appear smaller.
2. Obtain color swatches or color cards from your paint dealer and tack them to the walls you are planning to paint. Check these colors under both daylight and artificial light.
3. Blues and greens are cool colors. They can give the feeling of peacefulness and tranquility.
4. Reds and yellows are warm colors, and give the feeling of closeness and excitement.

5. Painting radiators, pipes, woodwork, and trim the same color as your walls will de-emphasize their presence; painting them contrasting colors will make them stand out, making the room seem smaller.

PAINT: HOW MUCH AND WHAT KIND

After you decide what color will be best for your walls, estimate the amount of paint necessary for the job. The formula for computing wall area is length multiplied by height. Calculate the area of all walls and subtract the area of doorways, windows, and any other openings. The resulting figure will be the total area you will be painting. When you shop for paint, check the back labels; there should be an approximate coverage figure for each kind of paint. Usually, 1 gallon of the better latex paints will cover approximately 450 square feet. That's an average room, 12 by 10 by 8 feet high. If you have any doubts, ask the paint salesman.

For the homeowner, there are four types of paint to choose from, each with properties suited for specific purposes:

Latex is the easiest type of paint for the nonprofessional to work with because it has a water base and dries in a few hours. The finish of latex paints is comparable to that of oil base paints. Latex paints can produce flat, semigloss, and high gloss finishes. There is quite a variety of standard colors, and there are hundreds of custom color mixes available, so you should have no problem obtaining the color you have in mind for your home. Painting tools and equipment can be cleaned with warm soapy water *before* the latex paint hardens. Odor free and fast drying, latex paints are the homeowner's answer to easy, quick painting.

Oil-base paints were once considered the only paint that would hold up under any type of wear. Most oil paints have a linseed oil base to which a pigment (color), drier, and thinner have been added. Drying time is at least 1 day and often longer. Oil-base paints are usually thinned with mineral spirits to keep the paint at the right consistency. The same thinner can be used to clean the tools and brushes.

Enamel paint is varnish with a pigment. The varnish gives a hard, glossy finish, but it is clear, so a pigment must be added for color. The result is a finish that is durable and glossy.

Alkyds are similar to latex paints in application but are more durable and more resistant to abrasion. These paints come in three types of finishes: flat, semigloss, and glossy. Alkyd paints are often used by commercial painters where a tough finish is required. Alkyds dry faster than oil-base paints, but slower than latex. Clean up tools and equipment with solvent or turpentine.

For a transparent finish over wood surfaces, where the natural wood tones are to be protected, the homeowner can use varnish or polyurethane. Polyurethane is an excellent finish for areas that will be exposed to a lot of traffic; it has an outstanding abrasion resistance and comes in semigloss (matte) and high-gloss finishes. Varnish provides a hard, glossy finish that will stand up well to moisture. Unlike polyurethane, varnish will not change the color or tones of the natural wood.

When deciding what type of paint to apply to your walls, consider the area carefully. In low traffic areas (bedrooms, living rooms, and studies), it is safe to use a flat latex paint. In areas of high moisture, such as a bathroom, kitchen, and laundry, use either an enamel or alkyd paint. These finishes will provide a finish that can be easily cleaned and will look fresh for years. In high traffic areas (hallways, playrooms, children's rooms, and dens), use oil base or alkyd paint.

Generally a primer is not necessary when a wall has been previously painted. However if the surface is new or the bare wood or wallboard is exposed or patching (with wood filler, plaster, or joint compound) has been done, the area should be primed. Peeling paint, stains, or water marks should be sanded and primed before a fresh coat of paint is applied. Primers will prevent the problem from recurring and will provide a good surface for the finish coat. Masonry and metal surfaces should be primed and sealed with an appropriate primer sealer before the finish coat is applied.

TOOLS

Paint brushes are like any other tool: If you buy good ones and take good care of them, they will last a long time. I have several high-quality brushes that I have been painting with for over 5 years.

Brushes range in price from 99c to $8 and up. For the average homeowner who paints occasionally, I recommend the medium priced brushes, in the $4 to $6 price range. Brushes in this price category will have strong handles, thick tapered bristles, and plenty of durability. Use nylon bristle brushes for latex paint and pure bristle brushes for oil, alkyd, varnish, and polyurethane paint.

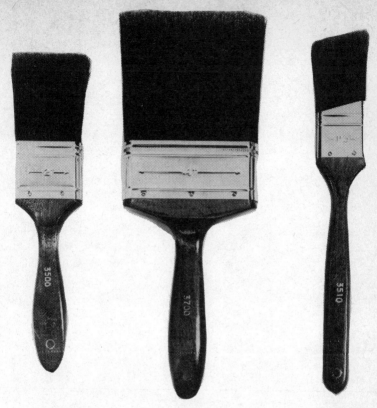

Fig. 3-1. From left to right, a sash brush, a wall brush, and an angular sash brush. (Courtesy National Paint and Coatings Association)

You will need at least two brushes for any wall painting job. One should be large, 4 to 5 inches wide, for large areas. The second should be small, 1 to 2 inches, for trim, windows, and detail work (Fig. 3-1).

The *roller* is the best invention for the painting world since paint itself (Fig. 3-2). A roller enables you to paint large areas with great speed. Texture of the painting surface does not matter; you can get roller sleeves that will cover any type of area, from flat and smooth to rough and porous. When buying a roller, choose one that has a strong handle with female threads in the butt end. The threads will enable you to attach an extension handle. Of course, you will also need a roller pan to hold the paint.

Roller sleeves, or covers, come in many types and textures. Choose one that is best suited for the particular wall surface you are

Fig. 3-2. A paint roller can save you hours of toil. (Courtesy National Paint and Coatings Association)

painting. Bushy roller covers will enable you to cover porous areas, because they hold more paint. Shorter nap rollers are for flat, nontextured surfaces.

You will also need a *paint scraper* or *putty knife, sandpaper, steel wool,* a *drop light* (to illuminate the surface), a *hammer* and *nailset* (for setting nails that have worked out), a *screwdriver* (for removing light switch plates and opening paint cans), *drop cloths* or *newspapers,* a *stepladder, rags, old clothes*, and a *hat* to protect your hair. Besides the paint and primer you will need some Spackle or patching plaster and turpentine or brush cleaner (for all paints except latex). If you are using latex paint, cleanup is with warm, soapy water.

SURFACE PREPARATION

The first step is to move everything out of the room that can be moved: furniture, rugs, lamps, pictures, curtains, etc. It's a good idea to vacuum the room before you start painting, but you can wait until you have cleaned and repaired the surface of the wall.

Look over the entire wall; there might be dark spots around radiators and heat registers, water marks around windows, peeling and blisters, cracks, and holes. Before you can paint, all these problems have to be dealt with. The following information will serve as a quick guide to solutions.

Problem	Remedy
Grime, grease, or dirt	Clean with household cleaner.
Holes	If they are small, fill with plaster and sand when dry; prime the area.
Cracks	Patch with plaster, sand, and prime the area.
Scales, Blisters, or Flaking	Scrape affected area, sand smooth, and prime the area.
Visible Nailheads	Set with hammer and punch, fill hole with plaster, sand when dry, and prime the area.
Watermarks	First determine cause; usually caulking is needed on exterior. Once problem has been corrected, sand and prime the area.
Stains	Sand and prime the area.
Mildew	Scrub area with strong household cleaner. When dry, prime the area.
Loose Paint	Scrape all loose paint, sand, and prime the area.
Dents and Nicks	Fill with plaster, sand when plaster has dried, and prime the area.

After the problems have been corrected, vacuum the room to remove all dust and dirt. Then lay down drop cloths and newspapers to protect your floors or carpeting. If there is any furniture that you couldn't move out of the room, cover it. Before you open the paint, make sure there is adequate ventilation; open windows or doors, to help keep air circulating in the room.

PAINTING: HOW IT'S DONE

Open the can of paint and stir the paint thoroughly. If you estimate that the walls will take more than 1 gallon, box the paint. That is, pour *all* the paint into one large container; mix it thoroughly. This procedure will assure a uniform color. I have found that a 5-gallon pail will hold more than enough paint for several rooms. After you have boxed the paint, pour it back into the gallon cans; seal up the containers that you won't be using for a while.

Begin painting where the wall meets the ceiling and paint a 3- to 4-inch strip along the top of the wall.

In this way, paint all around the room. Next, paint around the windows, doors, and light switches. Then paint the corners (from ceiling to floor) and the molding where the wall meets the floor (unless you are planning to paint it a different color or finish). Paint in careful, even strokes. The brush strokes should not be pronounced, and the original surface should be covered completely.

After you have roughed out the room with the brush, begin working with the roller. Pour enough paint into the roller pan to fill the bottom section. With the extension on the roller, run the roller down into the pan until it just touches the reservoir of paint. Run the roller back up the pan and work the paint into the nap of the roller (several dips into the paint will be necessary to evenly coat the roller). Place the roller against the surface to be painted and begin rolling vertically for about one foot, then roll downward. Roll up to the area that you covered with the brush and down to the floor. Apply the paint evenly. Recoat the roller in the pan often and the finish will be uniform. Failure to recoat the roller often enough will cause unpainted spots, or "holidays." Touch up areas that you missed while they are wet.

After you complete one wall, look over your work. Check for holidays and coverage of repaired areas. You cannot actually tell if the paint will cover until it is dry, but you can spot mistakes. If the first wall is done to your satisfaction, begin work on the next wall and continue until it is completed. Work with the roller in this way until the entire room is finished.

When you have completed the entire room, let it dry. If you are using latex paint, the waiting time will be only a few hours. After the paint has dried, look over the work and check again for holidays. Check for coverage. If you can see the old paint through the new, you will have to give the walls another coat. Two coats should cover even the darkest painted wall. It takes at least 24 hours for any paint to become hard, and some paints will take even longer. It is a good idea not to hang pictures or drapery for at least 24 hours.

If you have been using latex paint, the cleanup will be with warm, soapy water. If you have been using other types of paint, follow the cleanup directions on the paint can.

Doors and windows should be given a fresh coat of paint or varnish when you paint the walls. Woodwork, baseboard, and trim should also be painted at this time. If you have a natural wood finish on the existing woodwork, consider well before you paint it. Paint goes on easy, but is generally hard to remove. Before you cover any natural wood with color, make sure that's what you want.

Most woodwork will have a gloss to it and will not take new paint unless it is sanded first. Steel wool works best and will reach into indentations and crevices. After you have taken the sheen off the woodwork, wipe it down with a damp rag to remove dirt, sanding dust, and steel wool particles. Use a small brush on the woodwork and paint carefully. Straight lines will blend in well with the finished room, but a shabby paint job on moldings, windows, and doors will stick out like a sore thumb.

When you paint doors, prepare the surface by sanding and wiping clean. Then begin painting indentations, corners, and molding. Don't put a heavy coat of paint on the edges of the door or it may not close properly later. A careful, steady hand is necessary to paint around door hardware. Take your time. If you should slip and paint the lock or knob, wipe off the paint immediately. Doors will usually require two coats of semigloss paint. For best results, wait 24 hours before applying a second coat and lightly sand before applying that coat.

Painting windows requires patience, a steady hand, and a small brush. Begin by removing any loose paint. In areas of high moisture (e.g., bathroom or kitchen), you will probably find that mildew is present. Correct this problem by cleaning off the affected area with steel wool and a household cleaner. Prime the area and paint with a seimgloss paint after the primer has dried. Pull the upper sash down slightly and paint the sash edges, then paint the frame around each pane of glass. Take your time and wipe any paint off the glass as you go along. After you have painted the upper sash, begin work on the lower sash. Raise it slightly and paint the sash edges, then paint the frame around each pane of glass. After the lower sash has been painted, paint the window frame. It should take you about 1/2 hour to paint an average size double-hung window. Check your work and make sure you are satisfied with the results of your efforts. Remember that if you apply too much paint to the edges of the sashes, you may have a sticky window that will require Charles Atlas to open. Two light coats of paint on windows are always better than one heavy coat. If, after the paint has dried, you find that you have painted the windows shut, run a knife blade between the sashes and the frame; this should cut the seal.

Chapter 4
Textured Walls

There are several reasons for adding texture to walls. Textured walls can add to the decor of your rooms by creating a certain flavor—Spanish, Italian, South of the border, Tudor. Textured walls are intrinsically interesting—they are three dimensional, which means they have color *and* shape.

Adding texture to a wall usually involves applying a coating of plaster, joint compound, or sand paint. Generally, while the coating material is still wet and movable, a texture is applied. This texture can be added with a roller, a paint brush, burlap, a screen, a piece of wood, a trowel, a comb, or anything else that your imagination can come up with.

Sand paint can be applied and left as is. The sand in the paint will create a texture that is grainy (Fig. 4-1). If your walls have holes, cracks, etc., the solution lies in using a heavier coating material: painter's plaster or joint compound. Originally developed for patching problem walls and sealing joints in wallboards, these materials will enable you to add some heavy texture while curing the problems of your walls.

SAND PAINTING

Sand paint is the quickest way to add texture to your walls. Sand paint is just that—paint with fine-grained sand added. When you are working with sand paint, or any paint for that matter, the finished job can only be as good as the surface preparation. Sand paint will cover

Fig. 4-1. A wall covered with sand paint. (Courtesy PPG Industries)

hairline cracks and mask small nail holes, if properly applied. Large holes and cracks must be filled *before* applying the paint. Patch problem areas with Spackle. It is not usually necessary to prime patched areas; the sand paint will mask the repair.

Loose paint should be removed and the surface should be sanded before painting. Exposed nailheads, metal lath, and other base metal should be primed with a suitable metal primer before painting with sand paint. If they are not, the metal surfaces will "bleed" through the finished job. Old wallpaper, ink, crayon, and all types of stains should be primed before the painting begins. If you are in doubt about a surface's ability to show through the finished job, you should prime.

Working with sand paint is similar to working with any other latex wall paint; sand paint, of course, is a little thicker and will not cover as much area. Surface preparation should be the same for this type of painting.

The tools and equipment you will need to cover a wall with sand paint are:

> *Drop cloths*
> *Roller handle sleeve*—designed for sand paint

Extension handle Pan
Two paint brushes
Stepladder
Patching plaster
Sandpaper
Putty knife
Damp rag—for correcting errors
Sand paint—and tint, if you want a color other than off white

As with any painting job, it is best to clear the furniture, rugs, paintings, lamps, and other movable objects out of the room before surface preparation begins. After the room has been cleared, cover the floor with drop cloths. If you don't have drop cloths, or old sheets, lay newspapers down, but you should tape the edges of the pages together to prevent spreading.

After the surface has been patched, repaired, and primed, where necessary, begin painting with a brush. Paint all areas that cannot be easily covered with a roller.

One gallon of sand paint will cover about half the area that a gallon of conventional latex paint will cover. When sand paint is applied to a surface, the paint will penetrate *into* the surface but the sand will remain *on* the surface. The sand is held on the surface by the paint. What you end up with is a textured surface. The degree and type of texture will depend on how much sand paint is put on the surface and what has been done to the surface after the paint has been applied. For example, you can paint walls with a large paint brush, then when the paint dries, brush strokes will be very apparent.

When you have painted all the hard-to-reach areas, begin painting with a roller. Fill the bottom of your roller tray with sand paint. Attach the extension to your roller handle, slip on the roller cover (designed for sand paint), and begin rolling the roller down into the tray. Then roll the paint onto the wall. Try to cover areas approximately 2 by 3 feet. This small area will enable you to coat the entire wall with enough sand paint to work with later on.

Remember that sand paint will dry rapdily. If you are painting large wall areas or several walls, work in sections. The paint will still be in a workable state and you will be able to work in some texture. If you are painting a long wall, start in the middle of it and roll out a block 8 feet wide, from ceiling to floor. Create the texture you want and then begin painting a new block about 8 feet away from the fresh paint, working toward the fresh block of paint. When you reach the first painted area, it should be dry. Then you can apply texture to the freshly painted section. Work in this way until the entire wall has been covered and textured.

If you are painting a room with average dimensions, paint and texture one wall at a time, always applying texture before the sand paint has dried.

Sand paint doesn't lend itself to being textured with very many tools. In fact, about the only tools that can be used effectively to add texture to a freshly sand painted wall are paint brushes, textured rollers, and wall paper brushes. The use of a paint brush will give you a sweeping texture as wide as the paint brush. If you are using a 4-inch brush, for example, you will be able to add 4-inch texture strokes to the wall. If you are painting a large surface, it is some-times best to paint the entire wall with a wide brush and add texture as you go along. But adding texture with a brush can be tricky; if the strokes aren't uniform, the resulting texture may be sloppy.

To get the most uniform texture, paint with a textured roller. Textured rollers come in several types, from rollers with a short nap to bushy napped rollers. Rollers are also available with uneven nap which will cover a wall with a texture that is uniform but not flat. Short-nap rollers will give a texture that is relatively flat. Long nap rollers will give a texture that is almost flat but will coat the surface heavier than short-nap rollers. You can also paint a section of wall with a long-nap roller and, while the surface is still wet, sweep on a texture with a wallpaper brush. A wallpaper brush will give a texture that is wide, usually 12 to 18 inches.

Texture can be in the form of long sweeping lines (vertical or horizontal), swirls, long (or short) sweeping curves or arcs, and just about any design that your imagination can come up with.

Probably the best example of heavy texture on walls is stucco. Stucco walls are rough textured. There is usually a well defined pattern to any stucco wall, and this pattern contributes to the overall spirit of the room. With the use of painter's plaster or joint com-pound, it is possible to create a stucco texture that protrudes up to 1/2 inch.

Painter's plaster is sold in powder form and must be mixed with water before application. Setup time is about 10 minutes, so it is advisable to work quickly and with a small batch of the mixed plaster.

Application is simple with a large hand trowel and a pallet. Plaster is not generally recommended for concrete walls, but it will effectively cover just about any other surface. If the wall that you are planning to cover with plaster is cracked or marred, do the repair work first. Use painter's plaster for any extra large repair work. Remember, two light fillings are much better than one big glob. Allow sufficient time for the plaster to dry before the second application and wait until all the repaired surfaces are dry before applying the texture coat.

Very small cracks and holes need not be repaired before plastering the entire wall; they can be filled as you apply the texture coat.

All stains, bare metal, bare wood, and dark paint should be primed, for it is possible that these areas will "bleed" through. Also, an unprimed surface will many times not take plaster well or the plaster may crack and fall off later. The older painter's rule is handy here: when in doubt, prime.

After all large cracks and holes have been filled, mix up 1 or 2 pounds of the plaster by adding water until the mixture is firm but workable. Transfer the plaster to the pallet. Begin applying the plaster at the highest point on the wall, where the ceiling meets the wall, and work across about 2 feet and then down. Working in small areas such as this will give you enough time to cover the wall and add texture. While the plaster is still wet and workable you can add any texture you want. Any texture or marks you add will remain as lasting impressions when the wall dries.

Joint compound can also be used to create a stucco wall finish. Joint compound makes a fantastic texture medium, and because it takes several hours to dry and harden, it is extremely workable. Personally, I feel that joint compound is the best material for adding texture to a wall.

Joint compound is available in 5-gallon cans, and coverage is about 400 square feet, depending on how thickly the material is applied to the wall. Before applying joint compound to a wall, the surface should be painted white. This will prevent any color from bleeding through the finished texture. The usual priming and repair work should be completed *before* painting. After painting, apply the joint compound. Open the premixed compound and place a few pounds of the material on your pallet. Begin working at the top of the wall and work across and down, buttering the compound on in even strokes. After you cover a section of wall, say 3 or 4 feet wide, you can add texture or leave the "buttered on" look.

After you have applied the texture material to the wall, you can use a damp roller to flatten or play down the texture. Short-nap rollers will give you a flat texture with tiny bumps and indentations, very much like sand paint. Long-nap rollers will give a somewhat coarser texture. You can tie a piece of rope around the roller cover and roll on a texture that will resemble segmented lines.

The same putty knife, trowel, or spatula you use to apply the texture material to the wall can be used to add an interesting pattern to the wall. The texture material can be buttered on with a narrow-bladed putty knife using short strokes to give one type of texture, or a broader tool can be used with longer strokes to give another type. The use of a notched trowel will give still another type of texture. The different types of texture that can be added with small hand tools is limited only by your own creativity.

Wet burlap can be pressed onto the wall after the texture material has been applied. Just press it on and peel it off, the texture that remains will be subtle and unusual.

You can add texture with just about anything—with rakes, combs, pieces of weathered wood, brooms, woven straw mats, boxes, even your fingers.

Chapter 5
Wall Graphics

Wall graphics are supersized wall paintings, in dazzling colors. Wall graphics are the look of today. Bold bands of color sweep across walls, around corners, and off into the next room. They climb walls, across ceilings, and down the opposite wall where they might meet a piece of contemporary furniture. The wall graphic might take the shape of a gigantic half-circle or any other easily recognizable design.

Wall graphics are actually an outgrowth of the pop art movement that shook the world of design in the last decade. They have the ability to communicate ideas and personal feelings to anyone exposed to them. They can become extensions of your imagination, and this is part of their appeal.

THE POSSIBILITIES OF GRAPHICS

Before you begin to cover the walls in your home with giant lines, circles, and other geometric shapes, it might be a good idea to do one or two smaller graphics in an area that needs "something" to make it more interesting, perhaps a spare bedroom or an upstairs hallway. Live with this graphic for a while. Then if you decide that you want to live with more graphics around the house, plan, design, and paint others.

Graphics have the power to change the appearance of space through the optical distortion of design. Light switches, air-conditioning vents, heating pipes, and radiators can be made to "disappear" by running bold stripes or designs right across them. To make a discolored section of wall disappear, paint a large, bright square or circle over it. This treatment of the problem area will focus attention on the design and not the problem. Strategically placed curves and stripes "wipe out" the true proportions of a room and instill fresh life in lifeless spaces.

Graphics can create special moods or effects. Create the sensation of movement by painting colorful parallel stripes diagonally along the walls of a stairwell. Remember, any break in a pattern of straight lines will convey this feeling of movement. Working arrows into graphic design, or breaking up any part of the design, will achieve the same effect. Use arrows in addition of a bold stripe to show direction. For example, have an arrow pointing to a light switch or have the light switch in the head of the arrow.

Game rooms or dens can become visually exciting if a parcheesi board, monopoly board, hearts, diamonds, spades, or clubs are painted onto the walls. Kitchen walls become more exciting when familiar objects, like strawberries or orange trees, are painted onto the walls. Decorate the baby's room with supersized names or numerals, or decorate with gigantic cartoon characters, teddy bears, or the Seven Dwarfs.

Wall graphics should be free flowing and do not have to be contained within one room. A graphic pattern can be allowed to flow from one room to another to tie the house together. As the design flows into the next room, the pattern can shift into an entirely new mood, maybe one related to the room's use. By using a design in this way, you can avoid the impression of rooms being isolated and unrelated.

Let your imagination soar when conceptualizing your design, then bring it back down to earth and move on to the practical side of graphics, the planning, drawing, and painting. Modern wall graphics rely on super-scale, hard-edge designs to convey a powerful impact. Avoid feathery edges; they tend to soften the design and dull the impact.

SURFACE PREPARATION

Wall graphics require the same surface preparations as regular wall painting. The surface must be flat and free from any loose or falling plaster. The boldness of graphic colors will hide, to a degree, some surface irregularities, but if the surface is not flat, it will be difficult to obtain clean, crisp lines.

Since graphics usually have sharp edges and bold colors, the wall that the graphic is painted on should not detract from the graphic. In fact, graphics are usually most effective if the wall itself is white. Therefore, after you clean, scrape, and patch the wall, give it a fresh coat of white paint. Flat white will usually provide the best background because most of the graphic paints are glossy. However, if you have real problem walls, glossy graphic colors will make the imperfections on your wall seem more apparent. In this case, you would probably be better off using a flat or semigloss graphic paint.

If your walls are in very bad shape, it might be to your advantage to recover your walls with gypsum panels before you attempt to cover them with a graphic. After all, you can't expect to cure broken down walls with a few coats of paint.

APPLYING WALL GRAPHICS

There are two methods used by professionals to get a design onto a wall. In the first one, a design on a wall, in a magazine, or on drawing paper is photographed. The picture is developed as a slide; the slide is then projected onto the wall; and the outlines are traced onto the surface. The colors of the design are filled in after the design is outlined.

In the second method, a scale drawing of the design is made on a piece of graph paper. Each grid square represents an imaginary square on the wall, say 1 square foot. The design is then transferred, square by square, onto the wall.

When drawing the design onto a wall, aim for perfect accuracy and hard edges. Use every helpful tool at hand—yardstick, level, chalk line, etc. Draw the design with a soft, well sharpened pencil. If you make a mistake or want to change the design after it has been drawn, erase with an art gum eraser.

Figures 5-1 through 5-4 are contemporary wall graphic designs. You can reproduce these or modify them to suit your fancy.

Stencils can be used for numbers and letters if the design is not too large. If an identical pattern or shape is to be used in several places, make a stencil or template of your own to insure uniformity.

The best tools for drawing circles are a pencil, a piece of string, and a nail. Tie the string to the pencil. Measure the diameter of the

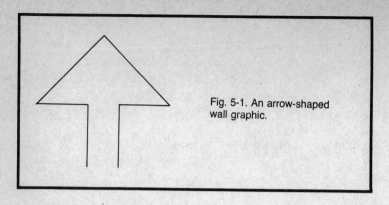

Fig. 5-1. An arrow-shaped wall graphic.

circle you want and mark its center on the wall. Make sure that the string's length is equal to the radius of the circle. Attach the loose end of the string to a nail, looping the string around the shank. Place the nail's point against the center mark and pencil in the circle, with the string taut, the pencil riding the perimeter of the circle. Of course, you can draw arcs in the same way.

Even the best job of tracing and spacing lines can be ruined by attempting to paint the edges of the design freehand. The solution is to use pressure-sensitive masking tape; this tape sticks on with a light touch and leaves no residue when removed. Outlining your designs with tape will help assure hard, sharp edges without paint brush slips. This tape can be purchased in a variety of widths in almost any hardware or paint store. One-inch widths are best for straight lines, and 1/4- to 1/2-inch widths are good for curved lines.

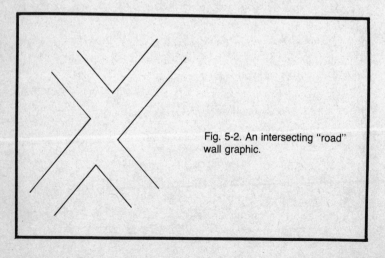

Fig. 5-2. An intersecting "road" wall graphic.

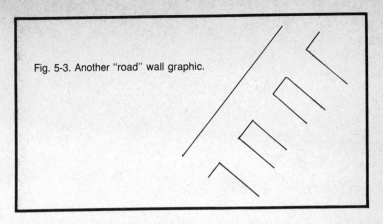

Fig. 5-3. Another "road" wall graphic.

There are a few tricks to using masking tape that will insure a neat, unmarred paint job. Don't apply the tape to background color on walls until the paint is at least a week old. If you tape too soon, the paint underneath may be lifted off when the tape is removed. Be sure that the walls are free of dirt and grime or the tape will not adhere properly.

When applying the tape, stretch it slightly and press its edge firmly into place. After you have taped a section of wall, check the tape for air bubbles and make sure that the tape is adhering firmly to the surface.

If your design runs across a corner, position the tape so you don't have to force it into the corner. This will insure that the tape stays in place until the paint is dry. Tape forced into a corner may pull out, causing the paint to smear or run down the corner.

To make sure that paint does not creep under the edges of the tape, press down the edges with the bowl of a spoon or any object of similar shape. This is one of the most important steps in the entire operation. A few smudged lines will spoil the effect of any graphic.

Tape should be removed as soon as the paint has dried to the touch. This will usually be within a few hours for oil base paints, even

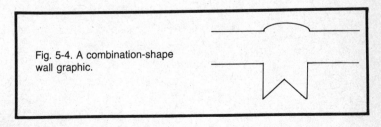

Fig. 5-4. A combination-shape
wall graphic.

sooner when latex paints are used. If the paint is allowed to dry all the way through before the tape is removed, cracking or splitting of the paint edges may occur. Never remove the tape by pulling it perpendicular to the wall; pull it slowly, at a slight angle and the edges should remain crisp and clear.

A two-tone wall graphic is one in which two different colors meet along a straight line. Oftentimes this means painting the top half of a wall one color, and the bottom half another. To achieve this effect, first use masking tape and paper to cover the bottom half, then paint the top half. First, the separation line is drawn across the wall; tape is then applied along the line where the top color is to stop. The top edge of the tape is pressed firmly to the wall so no smudging will occur. Paper for masking is attached to the bottom edge of the tape. The paper hangs down to shield against drips and overlapping paint from the paint brush. Remove the tape and paper when the paint is dry to the touch. Then, when the painted half has dried thoroughly (at least a week), again tape along the separation line, on the upper side. Paint the bottom half.

For creating narrow stripes, use the tape as a mask. Simply tape the area where you want the stripe to be; paint around the tape; remove the tape. You can also position two strips of tape and paint between them.

A variation on this technique is now possible through the use of automotive striping tape. This tape allows you to paint extremely narrow stripes because it is precut. After you lay the tape, you can peel thin, precut strips from it. Then you can paint over the tape, let dry, and lift the tape from the surface. The narrow stripes will remain.

Masking the insides of curves is a pretty simple job. Use a narrow tape; 1/4 to 1/2 inch works best because it is highly flexible and easy to bend into curves. Mask the inside edge of the curve with this narrow tape. Then, to the tape's lower edge (the edge away from where the paint will be applied), attach a wider tape. If necessary, attach masking paper to catch any overlaps or drips.

Tiny stencils can be cut out of a piece of masking tape. Then just lay the tape on the surface of the wall, paint the area that is visible through the stencil, and remove the tape when the paint has dried to the touch. Store-bought stencils are tricky to work with because their edges are difficult to attach to the wall; this will often result in smeared or running paint. Stencils actually work best when spray painted, but this can turn out to be quite a mess. All areas around the stencil must be masked with paper to prevent the sprayed paint from getting onto other areas. And, unfortunately, most canned spray paints simply don't work well on walls.

Graphics rely on striking colors to achieve impact, so be bold in your color selections. But boldness in color choice does not necessarily mean tastelessness. Get a few color charts and color chips from your paint dealer; take them home to get a general idea of just how bold your color choice is.

The effect you wish to achieve, the location of the graphic, and the condition of the wall on which it is to be applied will affect your choice of paint. Flat, semigloss or high gloss paints are all acceptable. Check with a reputable paint dealer for advice on paint selection. Surface imperfections are more apparent when covered with a glossy coating, while they are minimized when covered by a flat paint. On the other hand, glossy coatings are easier to clean.

Paint may be applied with a brush or roller or both. Personally, I perfer to use a small brush for the edges; this reduces mistakes.

Chapter 6
Brick and Stone

Today, designers and architects are using brick and stone to help create interior environments that have the look of the outdoors. The natural beauty inherent in brick and stone lends itself well to this purpose.

Though it is possible to install real brick and stone on interior walls, the cost, time involved, and experience necessary are limiting factors. The weight alone would be enough to collapse or at least sag a conventional floor. Yet it is entirely possible for the average home do-it-yourselfer to create brick or stone interior walls with a minimal amount of time and investment. I am referring, of course, to the wide selection of imitation brick and stone currently available.

THE FACTS ABOUT IMITATION BRICK AND STONE

When imitation brick and stone first became available, there was no doubt that these products were *imitation*. All imitation bricks looked alike—and looked phony. But imitation brick and fieldstone manufacturers have come a long way since the first reproductions came on the market. It is now possible to cover an interior wall with a fairly close representation of the real thing.

Imitation fieldstone, for example, is available in two types, several colors, and many patterns (Fig. 6-1). The first type of imitation fieldstone is made from a plastic material that is completely fireproof, so it can be used around fireplaces, behind kitchen ranges,

Fig. 6-1. A wall of imitation field stone. (Courtesy Barclay Industries, Inc.)

53

and almost anywhere else that has an above average amount of heat. Though the plastic type of fieldstone doesn't look exactly like real stone, it is a close representation and has the added advantage of being lightweight, easy to install, and relatively inexpensive. A wall in an average-size living room, for example, can be covered in less than a day, by one worker.

The other type of imitation fieldstone is a mixture of several stone and clay materials that have been molded and then fired in a kiln. The resulting fieldstone is very much like stone—hard, durable, and almost indestructible. Kiln-fired imitation fieldstone can be used almost anywhere.

If you prefer the look of brick, there is a great variety to choose from. As with fieldstone there are two basic types: plastic and kiln-fired. Imitation bricks are available in common brick red, used brick, white, gray, and black. You can buy them individually or as panels. Each panel will cover approximately 4 square feet. Panels interlock for a realistic effect (Fig. 6-2).

Imitation bricks have all the properties of imitation fieldstone: They are fireproof, durable, lightweight, and easy to install. The basic difference between the plastic and kiln-fired imitations is that the plastic versions are generally less expensive. And besides being cheaper and lighter than kiln-fired imitations, the plastic versions are easier to work with. Cuts can be easily made with simple hand tools. Kiln-fired bricks and stone, because of their hardness, require the use of special masonry blades for most cuts. Another point in favor of plastic brick and stone is that now most manufacturers are producing very realistic imitations of the real thing (Fig. 6-3).

If cost is a factor, you would probably be better off using plastic types of fieldstone or brick. If you are purist, however, I don't think you will be able to live with plastic. You will want to have the closest representation of brick or fieldstone, and that means the kiln-fired type. Most home improvement centers have a display showing the two types of imitations, both brick and stone.

The major companies that produce imitation brick and stone will he happy to send you brochures describing their products. The three major companies are: Barclay Industries, Inc., 65 Industrial Road, Lodi, New Jersey 07655; Masonite Corporation, Roxite Division, 7800 North Milwaukee Avenue, Niles, Illinois 60648; and Z-Brick Company, Woodinville, Washington 98072.

Fig. 6-2. A wall covered with interlocking "brick" panels. (Courtesy Barclay Industries, Inc.)

The plastic materials are installed very much like the kiln-fired materials. Bricks are applied to the surface of an interior wall that has first been cleaned, repaired, and covered with an adhesive. The bricks are applied in evenly spaced rows, with equal spacing between the joints.

Fieldstone is applied in a similar fashion except, because of the varied sizes and shapes, each piece must be fitted into a desired pattern. For this reason, working with fieldstone requires planning and a clear mental picture of the effect you are trying to create.

The adhesive used for both brick and stone is available in colors and textures that closely resemble cement mortar: gray, white, and black. After the entire interior wall has been covered with brick or stone, the joints between the pieces can be left as is or filled with some type of joint filler or grout. Most bricks are 5/16 inch thick, so unfilled joints will not look unattractive. But many homeowners perfer the look of filled joints. Filling the joints between the pieces does require more time, so plan accordingly.

Imitation brick and stone are commonly sold in boxes. On the average, one box of either brick or stone will cover approximately 6 square feet. Before you purchase the materials, plan the job thoroughly and estimate your material needs. Will you be filling the joints between the brick or stone? What color brick or stone will look best with your existing furnishings? Remember that you will need enough brick or stone for the job, plus an extra box to cover any errors. Joint mortar is available in tubes that will fit into any standard caulking gun. It is always best to buy extra materials to save you an extra trip to the store. If you have materials left over, they can usually be brought back. You will also need enough sealer to cover the entire wall.

SURFACE PREPARATION

Move all furniture as far away from the work area as possible. Cover the floor with a dropcloth or other suitable covering to protect against accidents. Begin by removing any moldings around windows and doors, light switch strike plates, picture hangers, and anything else that may be on the wall where you will be working.

Old, loose wallpaper must be removed, as should any loose or peeling paint. If the wall is covered with wallpaper that is in good shape, you don't have to remove it. You should, however, score the face of the wallpaper with a sharp knife so the adhesive will be able to

Fig. 6-3. These "brick" arches were built with plywood, hardboard, and Z-Brick.

57

do its job. Glossy painted areas should be sanded so the adhesive will stick. Mildewed areas must be cleaned with a solution of one part household bleach, and three parts warm water. Scrub the area with this mixture, let it dry, and then apply a coat of primer.

Small nail holes need not be filled, but anything larger should be repaired. Other holes and dents should be filled with Spackle. After the Spackle has dried, it should be sanded until the area is flat and flush with the rest of the wall. If any nailheads protrude from the surface of the wall, they should be countersunk.

If the wall you are planning to cover is extremely shabby, it may be necessary to cover it with new gypsum board.

The aim of surface preparation is to produce a uniformly flat, solid surface that will accept and hold a coat of adhesive and the brick or stone. The general condition of your walls and the surface preparation will determine how well the finished job looks and how long it lasts. After you have prepared the surface of the wall, it is a good idea to vacuum the area. This will prevent dirt and other foreign matter from getting into the adhesive. You might also consider wiping the entire surface of the wall with a damp rag. This will help to pick up any dirt on the surface and give the adhesive a bit of an advantage.

TOOLS

The tools you will need for installing brick or stone on an interior wall are as follows:

Notched trowel
3-inch-wide putty knife
Sandpaper or *Surform tool*
Hack saw or *circular saw*—with special masonry blade if you are cutting kiln-fired brick or stone
Stepladder
Level
Chisel hammer
1/2-inch dowel or *toothbrush*
Clean cloth rag
Caulking gun
String
Hammer and *nails*
Masking tape
Mortar bar—if you plan to fill the joints

APPLYING BRICK TO YOUR WALLS

Begin applying the adhesive at the top of the wall, close to the ceiling. Spread the adhesive over an area of approximately 4 square feet. Maintain an even thickness of 1/16 inch by using the notched trowel. Before you begin attaching the first row of bricks, stretch a string across the wall at a height where the bottom of the first course (row) should be. This can be accomplished by driving a nail at both ends of the wall, at the proper distance from the ceiling, and attaching the string between the two nails. Use this line as a guide for the bottom of the first row. Remove the string and nails *after* you have checked the first row.

Before each brick is set in place on the wall, apply a thin layer of adhesive to the back. Use the putty knife for this, but don't put too much on the back of the brick or the excess adhesive will ooze from behind when the brick is placed. Pretend that you are buttering a piece of bread as you spread the adhesive on each brick.

Press each brick firmly into place, wriggling it slightly to evenly distribute the adhesive and insure a solid bond (Fig. 6-4). If too much

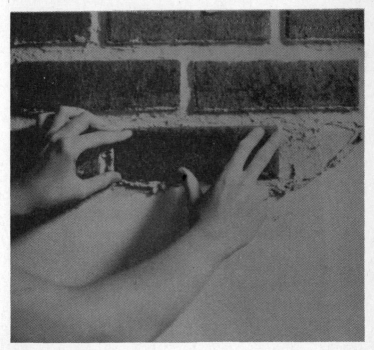

Fig. 6-4. Press the bricks into the adhesive. (Courtesy Z-Brick)

Fig. 6-5. Clear away excess adhesive with a small brush. (Courtesy Z-Brick)

adhesive is on either the brick or the wall it will ooze out. You can smooth in excess with a narrow brush after you have completed a few rows (Fig. 6-5).

Horizontal and vertical alignment is crucial to professional looking results, especially with the first row of bricks. You have some time before the adhesive hardens, so after you finish the first course, step back and examine your work. The first row must be straight because it is the guide for the rest of the courses. Use a level or ruler and the string guide to attain perfect alignment.

Even spacing all around each brick will help to give the finished job a uniform and natural look. It is a good idea to use some type of spacer or guide—a wooden dowel, for example—to keep the spacing around each brick equal. A piece of 1/2-inch dowel is much more reliable than the eye, especially when you are covering an *entire* wall. After each brick is set against the wall, insert the 1/2-inch dowel spacer between it and any adjoining bricks. If the spacing is off, reposition the brick. Once proper alignment has been attained, you can remove the dowel.

Begin the first course with a full brick. The first brick in the second course should be half a brick. Beginning every even numbered course with a half brick will insure broken joints between rows of bricks. Failure to use half bricks in this way will result in a finished wall with vertical columns of bricks. After all, you probably wouldn't want to have a wall with all the bricks in even, vertical columns, unless you had some special effect in mind.

Plastic bricks can be cut with a hack saw. Since you will probably have to cut several bricks in half, it may be helpful to first measure and cut one brick exactly in half. Use one of these halves as a guide for marking all the other bricks that need to be cut. This will insure uniformity.

You can also cut plastic bricks with a sharp ultility knife. Mark the back of the brick to the desired length and score the brick along this mark. Next, place the brick on the edge of a worktable, with the scored area lying along the edge. Use one hand to hold the brick on the work surface and the other to snap the brick. The brick will break along the scored mark.

The edges of all cut bricks must be smoothed over with sandpaper or a Surform tool. This operation is quickly accomplished and will insure natural looking rounded edges. If you fail to round off the edges of cut bricks when installed, the straight edge will stand out and detract from the overall effect of the finished wall.

Kiln-fired bricks are considerably harder than the plastic version, but they can be cut or broken to required size. To cut a kiln-fired brick, use a hacksaw or hand-held electrical saw with a special masonry cutting blade. If you use a hacksaw, mark the brick on the face and cut. If you use an electrical saw, mark the brick, fasten it down, and then make the cut.

Caution: When using an electrical saw to cut kiln-fired brick, wear some type of protective covering over your eyes.

Another method used for cutting kiln-fired brick is called controlled breaking. First, score the brick where you want it cut. You can score with a hacksaw. Next hold the brick in your cupped hand and tap lightly along the mark with a chisel hammer or with the edge of another brick. The brick should break along your score mark if you hit the mark squarely. Kiln-fired bricks are brittle, and you can use this hardness to your advantage when cutting or breaking. A pair of offset carbide-tipped tile nippers is a handy tool for removing small pieces from a brick. The nippers will come in handy if you have to fit bricks around an electrical outlet or switch.

Another method of cutting kiln-fired bricks involves the use of a pencil and a flat work area. First, score the brick for the cut. Place the score mark along a pencil lying flat on a work surface. Place one hand on one end of the brick and, with your other hand, force the other end of the brick downward. The brick will break along the mark because the brick is too brittle to bend.

After you have applied a few rows of brick, look over the work. Check the straightness of the rows, spacing between the bricks and rows, and any excess adhesive between the bricks. Any excess that may have oozed from behind a brick should be redistributed around the brick. Use a piece of 1/2-inch dowel or a narrow brush to spread the adhesive before it dries.

Check the faces of the brick for any adhesive. If you find any, wipe it off before it dries. If you fail to remove adhesive from the faces, it will be a noticeable flaw in the wall. You can remove any dried adhesive with some denatured alcohol on a soft cloth.

All corners will require special treatment, unless you are using special corner bricks which, in effect, wrap around outside corners. Inside corners present almost no problem at all. Butt the bricks of one wall up against the intersecting bricks of another and give special spacing care to the joint. Outside corners, however, are subject to wear and are more visible. One solution is to butt the bricks of one side of an outside corner with the bricks of the other side (Fig. 6-6). Then, after the adhesive has dried, sand, file, or cut off the overhanging bricks. A Surform tool is a handy item for cutting back overhanging plastic bricks.

Another treatment for outside corners involves mitering the edges of adjoining bricks to insure a tight fit. This method requires a bit of skill with a saw to get the edges to fit just right. Whichever method of corner treatment you choose, use more adhesive around the edges of the corner to help add extra strength to this area.

APPLYING FIELDSTONE TO YOUR WALLS

Fieldstone is attached to interior walls in much the same manner as brick. Adhesive is applied to the wall surface and to the back of each piece of stone before it is pressed into position.

It is a good idea to open several boxes of the fieldstone and mix the pieces together. This will insure that your wall will have an attractive distribution of brick tints. One box may have stone with a

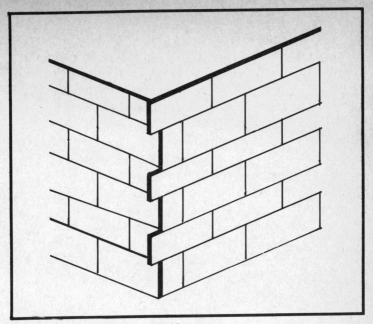

Fig. 6-6. Applying bricks to an outside corner.

gray cast, while other boxes may have stone with a slightly brown color. If you were to attach the stone as it came from the box, one section of the wall would have one tint; the rest of the wall would have another.

It might be helpful to arrange the pieces of stone on the floor or worktable *before* you attach them to the wall. By prearranging the stone, you will be able to develop the most attractive pattern for your wall and make best use of the pieces. Once you have a pattern arrangement laid out before you, you can transfer it to the wall.

Larger stones should be placed in the lower courses of the wall. Successively smaller stones should be laid from the lower courses to the top of the wall. Such an arrangement will give the wall balance and congruity.

The spaces between the stones should be as small as possible. But never lay one piece of stone on top of another without some kind of space between them. If there are spaces that are larger than they should be, fill them with small pieces of stone and joint filler.

As you lay out a pattern, try to always break the joints between the rows. There should never be any vertical spaces which run more than two courses.

Step back and look over the work often. If you should discover that the spacing is flawed, or that the courses are not straight (or too straight), correct these faults immediately. It generally takes a few hours for the adhesive to set, so if need be you can pull a few stones off the surface of the wall and relocate them. Remember that each piece of stone must have a thin coat of adhesive applied to its back before it's pressed into the adhesive on the wall.

Spacing between fieldstone pieces is just as important as spacing between bricks. For uniformity's sake, use some type of spacing guide, a piece of 1/2-inch dowel, for example.

One common problem that you should constantly be on the lookout for is excess adhesive around the stones. Correct this problem as soon as possible, before the adhesive has a chance to set and dry. As with brick, a piece of 1/2-inch dowel or a narrow brush can be used to redistribute the extra adhesive around the stone. If any adhesive should get on the face of the stone, it should be wiped off. Try removing it with a damp rag. If this doesn't work, try a rag dampened with denatured alcohol.

There should be very little cutting involved when working with fieldstone. Pieces should be arranged into a pattern, thus eliminating the need for a lot of cutting. However, sometimes a few pieces of stone must be cut to fit around electrical outlets or window and door openings. Plastic stone can usually be trimmed with a Surform tool or hacksaw. Kiln-fired stone can usually be broken with a chisel hammer. If only a small cut is necessary, you can usually remove small bits of kiln-fired stone with a pair of carbide-tipped tile nippers.

Inside corners present no problem when working with fieldstone. Simply butt the adjoining edges together and give a little attention to the spacing between the joints.

Outside corners, on the other hand, require more planning. Attach the stone to the wall as you normally would. As you approach the edge of an outside corner, stop the stonework 1 to 3 inches from the edge. By laying the stone away from the edge of the corner, you keep it from protruding past the corner where it can be easily damaged. You must paint the space between the end of the stonework and the edge of the corner with a color that matches the adjoining wall. This will make the space blend in.

Another possible treatment for outside corners requires a little woodworking. Attach outside corner molding or 1- by 4-inch boards

Fig. 6-7. A wall covered with stone and wood. (Courtesy Barclay Industries, Inc.)

over the edge of the outside corner, from ceiling to floor. Attach the stone to the wall, right up to the vertical woodwork. The addition of wood over an outside corner will insure that the stonework and the corner will remain protected against heavy traffic. You should paint or stain the molding or trim so it will match the other woodwork in the room. The addition of wood to a stone wall adds a distinctive charm to the room, and the wall will stand up much better to abuse (Fig. 6-7).

THE FINISHING TOUCHES

After you have completely covered an entire wall with brick or stone, you may want to fill the joints between the pieces. Filling the spaces between the pieces may not be necessary, depending on the type of brick or stone you use, the thickness of the pieces, and the overall effect you are trying to achieve.

If you decide that the joints must be filled, use special ready-mix joint mortar and mortar bag. A mortar bag is similar to a pastry bag. Ready-mix mortar that has been thinned slightly is scooped into the mortar bag. The back of the bag is sealed. Then the mortar bag is squeezed, forcing the mortar out of the special tip and into the spaces between the pieces of brick or stone. Work carefully and avoid getting any mortar on the face of the brick or stone. When the entire wall has been covered, go back over your work and smooth out any irregularities with a small brush. When smoothing out the mortar between the joints, work on the vertical spaces first. Then work on the horizontal spaces.

Whether you are installing brick or fieldstone, the job cannot be considered finished until the wall has been given a coat of sealer. The sealer will act as a protective shield and will make it easier to keep the wall clean. A minimum of one coat should be applied to all new brick and stonework (Fig. 6-8). In areas where there is an unusual amount of moisture or grease—behind kitchen ranges, for example—at least two coats of sealer should be applied. The sealer fills the pores in the stone and prevents dirt from becoming embedded.

PANELS

A type of paneling is now available which resembles stone or brick. One company, the Decro-Wall Corporation, produces panels

Fig. 6-8. Applying sealer to a new brick wall. (Courtesy Z-Brick)

that simulate natural cut stone and antiqued wood beams. Thse vinyl panels are self-adhesive and are called "Stone 'n Beam" (Fig. 6-9).

"Stone 'n Beam" offers do-it-yourselfers the natural look. The "stone" is weathered and textured. The "wood," built right into each panel, resembles the expensive beams so popular today.

To apply "Stone 'n Beam" panels simply peel off the backing paper and press onto the wall. The panels wipe clean with a damp cloth and have soundproofing and insulating qualities. They are available in packages of six panels, 12 by 24 inches. Each package covers approximately 12 square feet.

Another panel manufacturer, Masonite, offers a line of panels called "Roxite." Sixty percent of each panel is real crushed limestone, reinforced with fiberglass for added strength. Each panel measures 10 3/8 by 48 1/4 inches; there are 15 panels to a carton, which will cover approximately 50 square feet. Roxite panels are also available in "around the corner" versions, which are used to cover outside corners.

Roxite brick panels are intended for exterior or interior wall application. The only tools required to apply these premortared, interlocking panels are a hammer, hacksaw, saber saw or circular saw with special masonry blade. A hand or electric drill with a 3/16- or 5/32-inch bit may be necessary if the panels are to be applied to a plaster wall or similar surface. Use Roxite nylon fasteners if the wall does not have good nail-holding ability; that is, if nails aren't able to penetrate into a wood member. In general, this means that the nylon fasteners must be used when applying the panels to gypsum board, insulation board sheeting, masonry, and similar materials. If nylon fasteners aren't used on such surfaces, the wall should be furred out horizontally using 1- by 3-inch furring strips on 5 1/2-inch centers.

Mark all hidden framing members (studs) to facilitate nailing. Snap a level chalkline 11 lines up from the lowest corner (Fig.6-10). To make installation easier, these "brick" panels come with 10 1/4-inch starter strips. Apply the top edge of the starter strips 1/8 inch below the chalkline, nailing them to the base of the wall, 16 inches on center.

Then install the panels. If the installation involves outside corners, start by inserting the bottom grooved edge of an outside-corner panel securely into the starter strip. Nail the corner panel in place through the nailing guides on top of the panel using 1 1/2-inch ring-shank aluminum or galvanized nails (Fig. 6-11).

Install the first row of panels by inserting their bottom grooved edge securely into the starter strip. Nail them through the nailing guides on 16-inch centers using ring-shank aluminum or galvanized nails. Check the color of each panel as it is installed to take advantage of the variation designed into the panels. This will result in walls that closely resemble brick masonry.

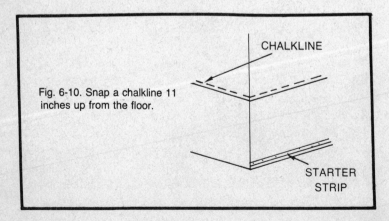

CHALKLINE

Fig. 6-10. Snap a chalkline 11 inches up from the floor.

STARTER STRIP

Fig. 6-9. Decro-Wall Corporation's "Stone 'n Beam" panels.

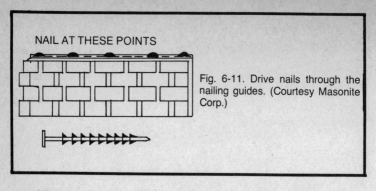

NAIL AT THESE POINTS

Fig. 6-11. Drive nails through the nailing guides. (Courtesy Masonite Corp.)

Make certain that the vertical joints between panels are tight. When applying panels at temperatures below 50°, allow an extra 1/16-inch gap at panel joints to allow for thermal expansion in warmer weather.

If panels intersect at an inside corner, butt one firmly into the corner and cut the other to fit against the first (Fig. 6-12). For accuracy, scribe a cut line in the panel.

When the panel course ends at an outside corner, the corner panel should be installed *before* the last panel. The last panel is then cut to fit, and the resulting joint is caulked with sealant or mortar.

All joints between panels should be caulked with sealant (Fig. 6-13). If the cut edges of the panels are exposed, fill the crevices behind the panels with crumpled paper, rags, or fiberglass insulation to within 1/4 inch of the cut edges. Then force Roxium Mortar or sealant into the crevices and onto the edges. After the mortar or sealant has cured for 2 hours, texture it so it blends in with the panel surfaces. Allow overnight drying. Color using Roxite touchup paint to match the panels.

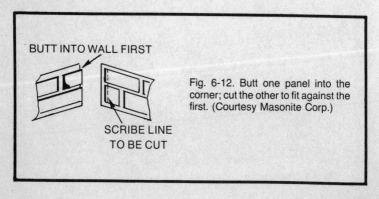

BUTT INTO WALL FIRST

SCRIBE LINE TO BE CUT

Fig. 6-12. Butt one panel into the corner; cut the other to fit against the first. (Courtesy Masonite Corp.)

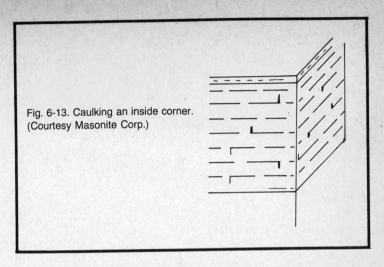

Fig. 6-13. Caulking an inside corner. (Courtesy Masonite Corp.)

If you like, you can add wood trim to the top edges of panels. Wide-width (4-inch) trim looks most attractive. Stain the trim a dark, natural color or paint it with high-gloss white enamel.

You can clean the panels with a brush, household detergent, and water. Most stains, grease, and grime will wipe off with a damp rag, providing the panels have been sealed.

Chapter 7
Paneling

You can make a statement about your lifestyle by covering the walls in your home with finely crafted prefinished paneling. A myriad of wood tones and patterns is available to suit your decorating flair and budget. Give new life to your tired, unfinished, or damaged walls with paneling specially crafted to withstand day to day abuses. Paneling is easy to install and practically maintenance free (Fig. 7-1).

THE FACTS ABOUT PANELING

Most paneling is plywood or pressed wood. Plywood makes the best paneling; pressed wood is used mostly on commercial walls. Paneling can be nailed directly to wall studs, but it's usually better to apply it over Sheetrock.

When selecting prefinished paneling, take into consideration the colors or tones of existing floor coverings, ceilings, and furnishings. There is a tremendous variety of paneling shades and colors to choose from. With a little planning and care, you can select paneling that will help to create a harmonious blend of colors throughout your home. Some lumberyards and paneling centers have brochures or samples of paneling that will help you decide which paneling you want.

If samples of paneling are not available from local lumber dealers, you can obtain brochures from Weyerhaeuser Company, Tacoma, Washington 98401 or Masonite Corporation, 29 North Wacker Drive, Chicago, Illinois 60606.

Fig. 7-1. By far, paneling is the least expensive, most mood-enhancing wall covering available. (Courtesy Barclay Industries, Inc.)

Table 7-1. Panel Estimating Table.

(For walls 8 feet 2 inches high or less)

Perimeter room (in feet)	4×8-Foot Panels Needed
12	3
24	6
36	9
40	10
44	11
48	12
52	13
56	14
60	15
64	16
68	17
72	18
92	23

Prefinished wall paneling is available in standard 4- by 8-foot sheets. Sheet thicknesses range from 3/16 to 1/4 inch. If the walls you are planning to cover are standard height, 8 feet, you can use the standard panels. If your walls are over 8 feet 2 inches high, you will have to order special-length panels or cut extra panels to make up the difference.

MATERIALS AND TOOLS

The first step in wall paneling, as with any remodeling project, is to plan the job thoroughly. Measure the length and height of the walls to be paneled. Calculate their area and subtract any space that will *not* be covered with paneling (windows, doorways, fireplaces, bookcases, etc.). In general you can deduct one-half panel for fire-places and doors and one-quarter panel for each window. To determine how many panels you'll need, divide 32 square feet (the area of one panel) into the calculated area. See Table 7-1.

When you calculate the number of panels you need, add an extra panel. An extra panel will compensate for errors in estimates and miscuts.

Molding and trim should be purchased at the same time as the paneling.

Humidity in most houses is very low, generally less than 4%. So panels will shrink once they've been in a room for a few hours, even if nailed to a wall. Stack them on edge for at least 48 hours before installation, making sure that plenty of air gets to each sheet.

Here are the tools used in paneling installations:

Hammer
Chalkline
Dividers or *compass*
Ruler or *measuring tape*
Level
Adhesive or *nails* or *both*
Padded block or *soft rubber mallet*
Drill
Saw—electric with plywood blade
Keyhole saw—for outlet holes
Surform tool
Saw horses—to provide an elevated cutting area
Putty knife or *scraper*
Sandpaper
Caulking gun—if adhesive is used
Miter box and *fine-toothed hacksaw*
Nail set
Utility knife

INSTALLATION

Paneling should be attached only to walls that are sound. If you are paneling a room that is below grade—a basement for example—or a room with masonry walls, you must first attach some sort of vapor barrier to prevent moisture from passing through the wall and into the paneling. Prefinished interior paneling is made with interior glue; therefore, moisture will cause it to deteriorate. A good vapor barrier to use is polyvinyl, made specifically for sealing out moisture.

Another solution to below grade moisture problems is to cover the walls first with water-resistant Sheetrock. Originally developed for high-moisture areas, this brand of Sheetrock will act as an effective vapor barrier and add strength and rigidity to paneled walls.

Fig. 7-2. Attach furring strips to walls that are in need of repair. (Courtesy Georgia-Pacific)

It's attached to wall studs in the same manner as conventional gypsum panels. All joints and nailheads are sealed, and then the paneling is attached over the Sheetrock using either the adhesive or nailing method.

Installing paneling above grade presents fewer problems, assuming that the walls are smooth, square, and sound. Most paneling manufacturers recommend that paneling be attached to walls that have first been covered with gypsum board. This type of installation will result in walls that are solid and almost soundproof. If, however, you want to cut costs, you can attach paneling directly to the wall studs or furring.

If all walls were true and sound, paneling would be a quick way to cover walls. However, most interior walls are not in good shape. If your walls are flawed (falling plaster, surface irregularities, holes, etc.), you must first attach furring strips to the walls. Furring strips are 1- by 2-inch lumber, usually rough cut.

Furring strips should first be attached vertically, spaced 16 inches apart, nailed to the wall studs that are behind the existing wall. Vertical strips should extend from the floor to the ceiling. You must also attach horizontal strips to act as nailers and to give the wall added strength (Fig. 7-2). The first horizontal strip should be nailed about 1 inch above the floor; horizontal strips are spaced approximately 1 foot apart. If you are attaching the furring strips to masonry walls, nail with masonry nails (Fig. 7-3). Attach the vapor barrier first and then nail the strips over it. Leave adequate space between strips for ventilation.

All existing moldings around windows and doors should be removed as the first step in surface preparation. Electrical outlet faceplates, picture hangers, and curtain rod brackets must be removed. If you are going to apply the paneling directly over an existing wall without attaching furring strips, make sure that the wall is reasonably flat. Sanding will often help to flatten small bumps.

After surface preparation, lay out the panels along the walls, arranging them for the most harmonious blend of color and grain. No two panels are exactly alike, so this initial arrangement is necessary to achieve some type of harmonious mix. After you decide where the panels are to go, number them on the back and stack them in a convenient place. Clear all furniture and moveable objects out of the room. Now you're ready to panel.

Fig. 7-3. Attach furring strips to cement walls with cement nails, bolts, or adhesive anchors. (Courtesy Georgia-Pacific)

There are two ways to attach prefinished paneling to interior walls: with nails or adhesive. Of course, it's possible to combine the two methods. The type of surface you will be covering will determine how you attach the panels. If you are attaching the panels directly to a flat wall surface, you can use adhesive. If, on the other hand, you are attaching the panels directly to wall studs or furring strips, you will have to nail. The nailing method is the simplest and quickest, but a combination of the two methods is the best.

Regular finishing nails can be used to attach the panels to the wall surface. Before the job can be considered finished, however, these nails must be countersunk and the holes filled with matching putty. You can simplify the nailing process by using nails with heads that match the color of the paneling. Colored nails eliminate the task of countersinking and filling the resulting holes. Use 1-inch nails for direct application to studs or furring strips and 1 5/8-inch nails for application over existing or Sheetrock walls.

The nailing method is as follows. Begin working in a corner by laying a panel up against the wall. Butt the panel edge against the adjoining wall and make sure that the other edge of the panel lies along the center of a stud or furring strip. Once joint location has been determined, paint a panel-colored stripe on the stud where the joint will be. Any gap between the panel edges will thus be less noticeable. Remember, the panel edges must align perfectly with the center of the studs.

Plumb the panel with a level and nail the panel from the center out. This method will insure that no bulges exist in the panel. Space nails approximately 4 inches apart along all edges; nail spacing for all other areas on the panel should be approximately 8 inches. Nail up all the other panels in a similar fashion.

As an aid to nailing through the panel and into the studs or furring strips, put pieces of tape on the floor or ceiling to mark the location of the studs or furring strips.

Often it is necessary to cut a hole in a panel to make the panel fit around wall protrusions like electrical outlets, thermostats, etc. The first step is to mark the protrusion surface with chalk or soft crayon and then place the panel up against the protrusion. Then tap the panel at the protrusion location; this will transfer the image of the protrusion onto the back of the panel. Next, use a utility knife to cut a hole in the panel around the image.

You can also make such cuts with a keyhole saw. First drill a hole in the center of the image large enough to take the blade of a keyhole saw. Then cut away.

Sometimes you have to cut off the top or bottom of a panel so it will be the right height. Often a room will have a ceiling height less than 8 feet and the panels will have to be cut.

First measure the height of the wall; if it is between 8 feet and 8 feet 2 inches, no cut is necessary. Mark the cut line on the panel with a scribe or pencil and straightedge. Cut the panel with a hand saw or electric circular saw.

If you use a hand saw, cut the panel with the face up. A circular saw, on the other hand, will rip the panel face unless the panel is cut with the face down. The cuts on the paneling will have smooth edges if a special plywood or paneling blade is used in the circular saw.

Sometimes you have to cut or panel lengthwise, from bottom edge to top. This type of cut is necessary when a full panel is not required. Mark the panel to the required width. Then, using either a hand saw or electric circular saw, make the cut.

To make a panel fit around a window or door you generally have to do a lot of cutting. Accurate measuring is important here. Measure the distance from the last applied panel to the door trim or to the opening if the trim has been removed. Measure up from the floor and down from the ceiling to get an accurate pattern for the cutout in the panel. Drill a 3/4-inch hole inside each corner of the cutout to provide a turning point for the saw. A keyhole or sabre saw, with a fine-toothed blade, is best for this type of cutting.

After a panel has been cut, the edges should be sanded to prevent splintering. Use either fine-grained sandpaper or a Surform tool. If, after the panel has been cut, it is still a trifle too big, the edges can be trimmed using the Surform Tool.

Irregular cuts are the biggest headache. When paneling butts up against a fireplace or brick wall, the panel must be notched so it will fit against this irregular surface. The simplest way to make such an irregular cut line on a panel is to hold the panel perpendicular to the irregular surface and scribe the cut line with a pair of dividers (Fig. 7-4). One point of the dividers follows the irregular surface; the other point scribes the pattern onto the panel. After the panel has been marked, it can be cut with a sharp utility knife or saber saw.

Waterproof panel adhesives, generally rubber base, are beaded onto walls from prepacked tubes with a caulking gun. Use panel

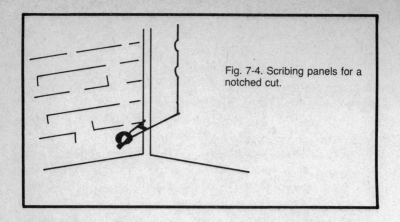

Fig. 7-4. Scribing panels for a notched cut.

adhesive with or without nails, according to the adhesive manufacturer's instructions on the tube. Usually, paneling is installed *after* the adhesive has become tacky. In questionable situations, such as installation directly to porous plaster, auxiliary nailing is required with any adhesive. In most cases you can apply panel adhesive directly to wall studs or furring strips. After each panel has been installed, tap it in place with a mallet or cloth-covered block to insure a good bond.

One paneling manufacturer (Weyerhaeuser) makes a high-strength glue recommended for use in installing panel materials, in either interior or exterior applications. Its versatility and superior bonding properties make it the ideal adhesive for the homeowner, the builder, or the shop fabricator.

Other recommended adhesives for paneling include four that require the use of some nails: PL-200 (B.F. Goodrich), Miracle #10 (Miracle Adhesive Corporation), Macco PA 12 (Macco Chemical, Division of Glidden), and 3M Panel Adhesive.

Panel adhesives that are recommended for use without nails are: Wallbond (Continental Chemical and Coating Co.), Panyleze (Panyl Corporation), Panelgrip (Columbia Cement Co.), Cordibond (McCordi Company), Full-O-Mite (H.B. Fuller Co.), Scotch Construction Adhesive (3M Company), and H. B. Fuller Tan Mastic BC 688.

Contact cement is not recommended for some types of paneling. Check where you purchase the paneling to be sure that the type you are using can be attached with contact cement. This type of adhesive will not work well on rough surfaces, such as most plastered walls, or over paint or wallpaper. If you remove paint from a wall in order to use contact cement, be sure to eliminate any trace of wax left by the paint remover by using painter's naphtha.

When installing paneling with contact cement, first be sure that the panel fits properly. Carefully follow the instructions on the cement can, observing any safety warnings. Use a 2-inch brush to coat faces of the furring strips or studs and the corresponding locations on the back of the panels.

When installing paneling directly on a smooth surface, brush the cement on the back of the panels in 2-inch-wide strips, around the panel perimeter. Paint on horizontal strips too, 12 inches apart. Brush cement on the wall surface where the cemented panel will join.

Install panels only after the contact cement has dried. Position each panel exactly, pressing an edge against the wall first, then swinging the rest of the panel against the wall for full contact. Place the edge of each subsequent panel against the edge of the previous panel before swinging it against the wall. Work carefully; you will not be able to move the panel once contact has been made. After each panel has been attached to the wall, insure solid bonding by tapping with a rubber mallet or padded block and hammer.

Adhesive that comes in tubes can be used to fasten panels to solid backing (Sheetrock, plaster walls, etc.) or to studs and furring strips. To attach paneling to solid backing, you must first make sure that the surface is sound and clean. If wallpaper is on the walls, remove any loose pieces. Old wallpaper in good condition can be left on the walls, but the face should be scored with a knife to insure a good bond. Begin laying panels in a corner. Apply the adhesive to the back of each panel and the wall surface.

Whether you're using cement or tube adhesive, panels are pressed against walls in the same manner: Press an edge into place, then swing the rest of the panel into position. But before you attach a panel, check it with a level to insure that it is square and true. Once you are satisfied with the position of the panel on the wall, you can drive two nails into the top of the panel for reinforcement. The nails can be covered later with trim.

After all panels are installed, reapply pressure to all areas of the panels to insure firm contact with the adhesive. To apply this pressure, you can use your hands, a rubber mallet, or a cloth-covered block and hammer.

Special attention should be given to all areas where panels meet. If you have applied enough panel adhesive, the panels should lie flat on the wall. But, if the adhesive was applied too sparingly or if the wall surface is not uniformly flat, you may have to drive a few nails to hold the panel flat against the wall.

To attach paneling to bare studs or furring strips with panel adhesive, apply the adhesive to the bare uprights in 3-inch ribbons. Adhesive should also be applied to any horizontal furring or studs. Special attention should be given to the areas where the panel edges meet the floor, ceiling, and other panels.

If a panel isn't square, or the top or bottom of the wall is out of true, use shims along the bottom edge of the panel to raise or lower it into proper alignment. Remember, panel edges should be aligned with wall studs, not with the floor or ceiling. Once the panel is square, drive two nails along the top edge of the panel to help hold it in place. Later these nails can be covered with ceiling molding. After the panel is attached, you can remove the shims.

TRIM

When all the paneling has been attached to the walls, look over the job. You may have some gaps at the top or bottom of the walls, outlet box openings may be a little large, corners may not be as tight as they should be, and there may be gaps around window and door openings. Trim, or molding, can help finish off a job that is not exactly right. Trim can also add a decorative touch to your walls. But you must work carefully for best results.

There are two basic types of molding available for the do-it-yourselfer: prefinished molding in either wood or vinyl and unfinished wooden molding. Both types are available in all the common sizes and shapes: outside corner, inside corner, base, cap, cove, stool, mullion, stop, casing, and seam. Prefinished molding can be installed quicker because there is nothing else to do once it is attached. Prefinished molding will match or contrast any paneling (Fig. 7-5).

The new polyvinyl prefinished moldings, which are available in wood-grained finishes and off-white, will provide a tough, durable trim around any paneling job. They are easier to work with than wooden moldings because they resist splitting, chipping, and warping. And they won't shrink at all because they are moisture resistant.

Look over the vinyl moldings when you are buying paneling; you may decide that they are right for your walls.

If you are not satisfied with the prefinished trim available, you will have to buy unfinished trim, then finish them yourself. Some homeowners prefer the natural wood finish on molding and trim. Though a natural finish requires more work, the results have a custom look not available in prefinished molding.

Fitting and installing trim around openings, walls, floors, and ceilings is an important part of any paneling job. The accuracy with which mating parts fit together will greatly enhance or detract from the finished paneling job.

To apply casing trim (Fig. 7-5) around a door, first select the necessary pieces and place them near the opening. Make sure that the bottom of the casing is square and will rest on the floor. Hold the side (doorpost) pieces in place and mark them where they will be cut (these pieces must be mitered on their top ends). Use a miter box to help you make an accurate cut. Nail the side pieces around the opening (with color-matched nails if you are using prefinished trim). Drive the nails only far enough to temporarily hold the trim in place; this will allow you to move it for a better fit later on. Now measure and cut the top (lintel) trim. After all the pieces are cut and checked for fit, finish nailing all around the opening and countersink all nailheads. Window trim is installed in the same way.

Baseboard and ceiling trim should be installed around the entire perimeter of the room. The inside corners of the trim should be coped (cut with a coping saw); outside corners should be mitered.

The corners themselves should be trimmed too. To finish inside corners, use inside corner trim from floor to ceiling; outside corners are finished with outside corner trim.

Molding should always be installed as one piece. Sometimes, however, this is not possible. If the span is greater than the length of the trim you are installing, splice two or more lengths together. To splice lengths of trim along the same wall, make 45° cuts at the same angles on both pieces. After the molding has been nailed in place, the seam will be barely visible.

After all trim has been cut and installed, countersink all nailheads. If you are using natural (unfinished) wood trim, you must fill the nail holes with a matching wood filler. When the filler has dried, lightly sand the area with 3/0 sandpaper and apply a coat of

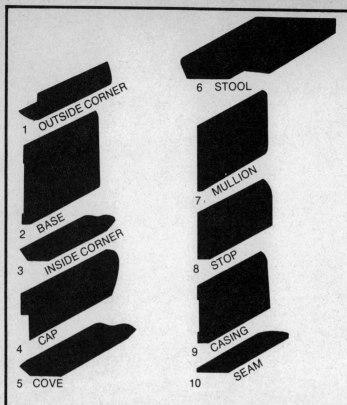

Fig. 7-5. Prefinished moldings. (Courtesy Georgia-Pacific)

wood sealer or stain. When this is dry, sand lightly and apply two coats of clear varnish or polyurethane, lightly sanding between coats. When the final coat has dried, you will have natural looking molding that will withstand moderate abuse.

After the trimwork is completed, look over the walls. Check the seams where panels meet; if you can see the wall underneath, run a putty stick down the seam to darken the area. (Putty sticks are available in matching colors.) Then rub the area lightly with a soft cloth to help blend the putty into the panel face.

PANELING MAINTENANCE

Quality, prefinished interior paneling will require minimum maintenance. The finish will resist stains, mars, and fingerprints. However, if scratches do occur, they can usually be removed as long

as they are not too deep. Use a clear wax on a damp cloth and rub the scratched area, along the grain of the panel. It may be necessary to wax the entire wall to insure uniform color. And waxing an entire wall will often restore paneling to its original condition. Deep scratches can often be remedied with the use of a color-matched putty stick.

Pencil marks, crayon marks and the like may be cleaned off with a damp cloth or, in severe cases, a mild detergent. Always wipe *with* the grain, and after the area is clean, let it dry and apply a clear, liquid wax. Never use an abrasive cleaner; the grit in these cleaners will scratch the finish. If you get paint on the paneling, remove it as quickly as possible with a damp rag. Most prefinished paneling will not hold up to paint thinners or solvents.

Panels exposed to the direct rays of the sun will gradually become lighter. So pictures and other objects hung on a paneled wall should be set off from the surface. This insures that light will be more or less evenly distributed over the entire wall. You can set picture frames away from the wall by attaching small blocks or nails to the back of the frame.

Chapter 8
Waterproof Walls

Waterproof walls are a necessity in at least one room in every home in America. Traditionally, the bathroom has been the room that receives the waterproof wall treatment. But waterproof walls are also common in the kitchen, laundry, and other rooms that require a special, attractive wall treatment. There are two ways in which a wall can be made waterproof: glazed ceramic tile and plastic-coated paneling.

THE USE OF CERAMIC TILE

Ceramic tile is attractive and traditionally popular in bathrooms all over the country. There was a time when only a limited variety of tile was available, mostly white. Modern tile manufacturers now, however, offer a vast selection of tiles in just about every color in the rainbow and in decorator designed patterns.

The photo of Fig. 8-1 shows the high-styled touch you can achieve with decorative tile. Note the accent tile in the counter surface. Another imaginative use of tile is shown in Fig. 8-2, where five individual motifs are brought together to form an integrated whole. In the modern kitchen/dining area, diagonally patterned tiles are juxtapositioned on the back wall to form a repeating "X" configuration with straight-set tiles. Under the cupboards, plain white tiles are placed with a diagonal laying technique. The work surfaces are formed by a consistent pattern of light colored miniatures. The snack surface matches the undercabinet design, except that the tiles here are horizontal/vertical rather than diagonal. Note that the floor kick-panel area is formed with a dark-tile strip, and the hex-pattern flooring simulates tile. Lots of tile here, but it doesn't appear overdone because a great deal of thought went into the overall coordinated effect.

Tile is water resistant and, if properly installed, water will never pass through the tile into the wall behind. Tile is also extremely tough; it is stain resistant and is one of the few wall coverings that can be scrubbed with an abrasive cleanser. It doesn't fade either. The only problem with a wall covered with tile is the joints between the tiles. The grout used to fill the joints will sometimes discolor if there are heavy concentrations of iron in your water. Grout will also discolor if it is subject to large amounts of grease, behind the kitchen range for example. Possible problems with grout should be anticipated and prevented by using special grout that is resistant to discoloration. There are several types of silicone grout on the market that will stand up to the toughest punishment.

There are two drawbacks to installing cermaic tile: cost and time. Tile is expensive, costing about $1 per square foot and up. You could spend a small fortune in no time at all. I have seen some beautiful, handmade imported tiles selling for $5 each. Obviously not for everyone.

The other drawback is time. Most tile comes in pieces that measure 4 1/4 by 4 1/4 inches and must be individually set. However, one company, American Olean, offers ceramic tile in sheets of 12 tiles. The sheets reduce installation time, but you will still have to do some cutting around fixtures. You can safely figure that it will take you about two days to tile an average sized bathroom.

WATERPROOF PANELING: AN ALTERNATIVE TO TILE

Another way to make your walls waterproof is to cover them with plastic-coated wall paneling (Fig. 8-3). Like other paneling, plastic coated paneling comes in 4- by 8-foot sheets. The panels are attached to walls with adhesive, and the joints between the panels are made waterproof by using special metal moldings which the panels fit into. Generally, the panels are two ply: 1/8-inch sheet plastic on a hard backing. This type of paneling costs around $12 per sheet at the low end of the price range.

Fig. 8-1. Decorative tile can cover a wall or counter or both. (Courtesy Tile Council of America)

Fig. 8-2. A kitchen decorated with five kinds of tile. (Courtesy Tile Council of America)

You don't have to be a master carpenter to install waterproof paneling, but you do have to be able to use a ruler because the panels must fit snugly into the moldings or water will sneak into the joints and slowly rot the subwall. If you install plastic-coated paneling over an existing wall that isn't square, you may run into serious problems

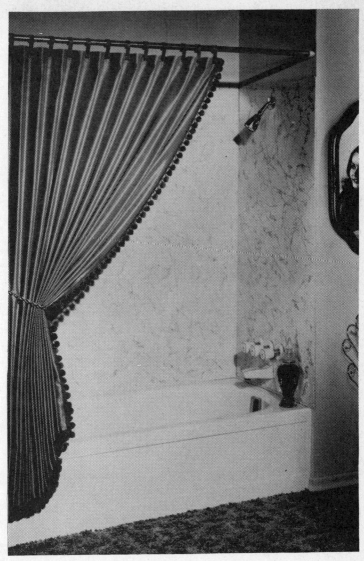

Fig. 8-3. Shower walls covered with colorful, watertight panels. (Courtesy Masonite Corp.)

when you try to make the edges fit tightly. But, if you follow the old carpenter's rule of "measure twice, cut once," you should be able to do the job correctly and end up with watertight walls.

Plastic-coated paneling is available in at least 50 different patterns and colors. Visit your local lumberyard or home improvement center and look over the selection. One company, Barclay, offers around 40 different styles plus matching moldings.

Plastic-coated panels are tough and resist stains, scratches, smudging, and scuffing. A damp cloth and a little elbow grease will remove most soil. Never use abrasive cleansers though or you will damage the finish.

Plastic paneling offers the quickest and least expensive way to make walls waterproof. If properly installed, the panels will provide maintenance-free walls that will stand up to most kinds of abuse. Paneling is also the best solution to old problem walls because you will be adding strength instead of adding weight, as in ceramic tile.

ESTIMATING YOUR TILE NEEDS

The amount of tile you will need to cover a wall will depend on the area of the wall. Tile is often used to cover a wall from floor to ceiling, but the job may be more effective if you cover only part of the wall, say to a height of 6 feet. Tile around a bathtub is commonly laid to 6 inches above the shower head, which is usually at a height of 6 feet. Tile behind toilets and on other walls is usually laid to about 4 feet high (Fig. 8-4). In the kitchen, tile is usually laid from the counter top to just below the cabinets.

The simplest way to determine the number of tiles you will need to cover a wall is to measure the length of the wall and divide by 4 5/16 inches (4 1/4 inches for the tile and 1/16 inch for the joint). This equation gives you the number of tiles you will need per row. Next, measure the height of the wall (or the height of the proposed tiled surface) and divide by 4 5/16 inches. This gives you the number of rows required. Round off both numbers to the nearest whole number and multiply them. The product is the number of tiles needed. Do the same computation for other walls. Add all the walls together and you will have a total tile figure. If you are using trim tiles (at the top or bottom of the wall), make the appropriate additions to your total tile figure.

Another way to give you a rough estimate of the number of tiles you will need is to first determine the length and height of the wall.

Fig. 8-4. Walls behind toilets and sinks need not be completely covered with tile. (Courtesy American Olean)

For every foot of length, you will need three tiles. For every foot of height, you will also need three tiles. Determine the approximate number of tiles you will need for both the length and the height; round off the approximations to the next highest number and multiply the two numbers. This will give you an estimate of the number of tiles needed. Remember that the work will go much quicker if you buy tile in pregrouted sheets of 12 tiles each.

If you don't want to be bothered with these calculations, simply measure the length and height of all the walls you want to cover and give your tile salesman these figures. He should be able to determine the number of tiles you will need to complete the job.

TOOLS AND MATERIALS FOR INSTALLING TILE

When your purchase the tile, buy the adhesive and grout. Buy one gallon of adhesive for every 50 square feet of wall space. If you are using ceramic tile sheets, you will need a few tubes of special grout to waterproof the seams between the sheets. An excellent type of grout is Dow Corning 784 Silicone Rubber Sealant. One 10-ounce cartridge will cover approximately 50 square feet of tile area.

The tools you will need to help you apply tile to your walls are:

Pliers or *tile nippers*
Level
Tile-cutting kit
3/16 Notched adhesive trowel
Hand caulking gun
Denatured alcohol
Ruler
Sandpaper, file, or *carborundum stone*

TILE INSTALLATION

The surface to be tiled should be structurally sound, with no lumps, holes, peeling or crumbling finish. If there is any type of wall covering on the wall, like the deteriorating surface shown in Fig. 8-5, it should be removed. Otherwise, your new surface will be attached from the underside from the moment it's installed. Glossy surfaces must be dulled by sanding. Any dust, wax, grease, or water-soluble paint must be removed. The wall should be stripped clean(Fig. 8-6).

Fig. 8-5. A "pitted" wall in a high-moisture area. (Courtesy American Olean)

Fig. 8-6. Stripped bathroom walls. (Courtesy American Olean)

There's no telling what you're apt to find under the old wall surface. If there are gaping holes, these must be filled so that a new, perfectly flat backup wall can be provided for the new tile you've selected. Did you notice the gaping cutout for the plumbing fixtures in Fig. 8-6? The photo of Fig. 8-7 shows how this situation (which is quite common, especially when you're dealing with older walls or paneling that was installed by a self-styled expert) can be corrected. Just cut a section of waterproof gypsum large enough to fit into the missing section. Note the smaller holes in the add-on panel which allow the plumbing fixtures to protrude through. The repair panel will be cemented into place.

After the surface has been prepared so that it is flat, clean and in sound condition, apply the adhesive to the wall with a notched trowel (Fig. 8-8). Until you become proficient at setting the tile, spread adhesive only on one small area at a time.

The following instructions apply to the installation of tile sheets as well as individual tiles.

Once you have covered a section of the wall with adhesive, begin setting the tile. Begin at the lowest point of the wall and work upward. Press the tile firmly into the adhesive (Fig. 8-9). Tiles (or tile sheets) should be butted together as tightly as possible. If you butt the tiles together carefully, the rows should be perfectly straight. However, it's wise to check the rows often with your level. As tile is applied, remove any excess adhesive that oozes from the joints. Excess adhesive may be removed with a cloth dampened with denatured alcohol.

For outside corners, begin tile installation at the edge and work away from the corner. If both sides of an outside corner are to be tiled, overlap one edge with the intersecting sheet, as shown in Fig. 8-10. All exposed tile edges should be finished glazed edges.

It is inevitable that you will have to do some cutting of tile, so it will be worth your while to have a tile-cutting kit. This kit will enable you to make straight cuts. Curved cuts can be done with a pair of tile nippers or pliers (Fig. 8-11).

To make a straight cut on tile, place the tile on a wood surface, as shown in Fig. 8-12, then using straightedge and scribe, score the glazed surface. Position the scored line directly along the edge of a board or table. Place one hand on each side of the scored line and apply pressure downward to break the tile on the scored line (Fig. 8-13).

Fig. 8-7. Inserting gypsum around plumbing fixtures. (Courtesy American Olean)

Fig. 8-8. Spreading on the adhesive. (Courtesy American Olean)

Fig. 8-9. Embedding the tile. (Courtesy American Olean)

An alternate cutting method is possible by scoring the tile on the glazed side with a glass cutter and straightedge. Then, with the glazed side up, position the scored line along a straight piece of wire resting on a table. A coat hanger will do. Snap the tile by pressing firmly on both sides of the scored line.

Whichever method you use to make a straight cut on the tile, care should be taken to protect your eyes from flying chips. Also, cut

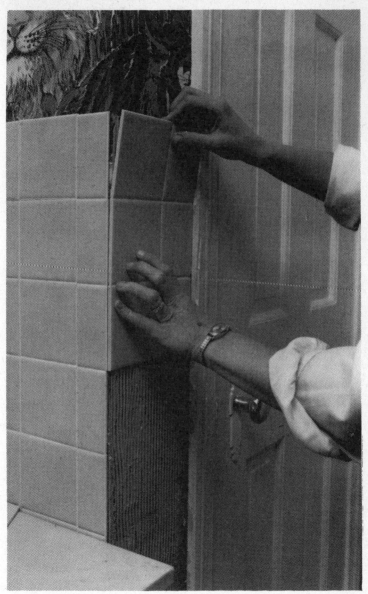

Fig. 8-10. Overlapping tile at an outside corner. (Courtesy American Olean)

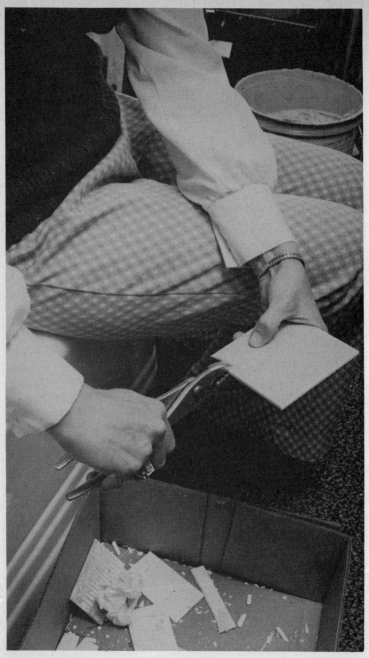

Fig. 8-11. Pliers can be used to "bite" off pieces of tile. (Courtesy American Olean)

tile edges are sharp, so be careful. Smooth cut edges with medium-grit sandpaper, a file, or a carborundum stone.

You will also have to make a few irregular cuts, around plumbing pipes for example (Fig. 8-14), or around built-in soap trays and the

Fig. 8-12. Scoring the glazed surface of a tile. (Courtesy American Olean)

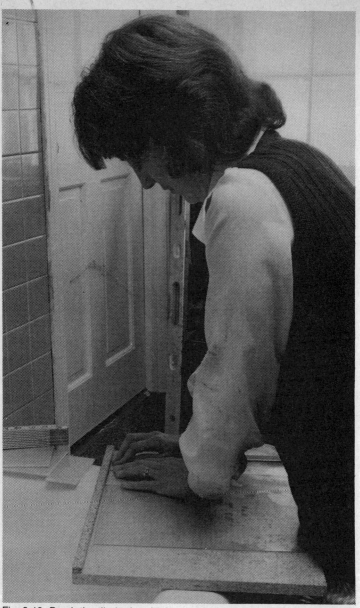

Fig. 8-13. Break the tile by hand, along the scored line. (Courtesy American Olean)

like. This is easily accomplished with tile nippers or pliers. Measure carefully where the tile must be cut and start from the edge of the tile, taking 1/8-inch bites until you have the right size hole. If the hole falls in the middle of the tile, first cut the tile in half, then take small pieces out of each side of the cut until you have the proper sized hole. If the cutout piece is at an edge, it's wisest to cut or nibble a section, then try the fit, repeating the process as often as necessary to get a good fit (Fig. 8-15).

After you have completed one wall, go back over the work and press the tiles into place with a board. This additional even pressure will help to assure that all the tiles are in the same plane.

After all the walls have been covered with tile you can install corner strips. Inside corner strips will provide a finished easy-to-clean corner and will become added insurance at this notoriously hard-to-keep dry area (Fig. 8-16). Corners are the toughest parts of a wall to keep waterproof.

After the wall has been completely tiled and the tile has set in the adhesive for the recommended time (this will vary from a few hours to 2 days), fill the joints between the tiles or tile sheets with grout. Tile sheets are pregrouted, but joints between sheets must be filled with grout. One of the best grouts available is Dow Corning's 748 Silicone Rubber Sealant. The directions on each 10-ounce tube do not apply to the installation of ceramic tile and therefore should not be followed.

Simply remove the nozzle from the rear of the tube and place it on the end of the tube. Put the tube in a caulking gun. Grout the joints, holding the gun at about the angle shown in Fig. 8-17. Work on one wall at a time, applying the grout to all joints, around fixtures, cuts, corners, and where the tile meets other surfaces (around the top of the tub for example).

Cheesecloth, wet with denatured alcohol, should be used to smooth the joints and remove any excess grout from the tile surface. Clean up as you work (Fig. 8-18) and try to avoid smearing tile surfaces with the silicone sealant.

After the walls have been grouted and the grout has dried—usually a day or so—you can polish the walls with a soft rag. Then they will be ready for use (Fig. 8-19).

Occasional maintenance of the cermaic tile and grout will be required. Normally, a damp cloth or sponge will restore the walls to their original gleaming surface. To remove stubborn marks, use any common household cleaner, such as Windex or Fantastic, followed by a final polishing with a clean paper towel. The beauty of cermaic

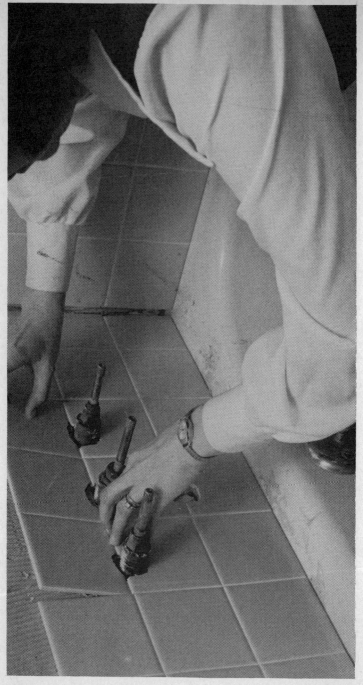

Fig. 8-14. Cut the tile so it fits around pipes. (Courtesy American Olean)

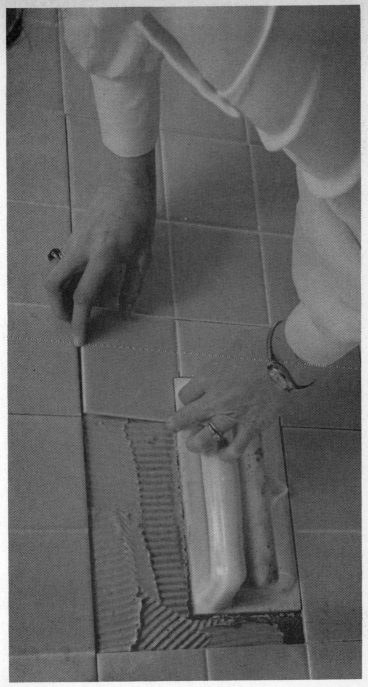

Fig. 8-15. Fitting tile around an obstruction. (Courtesy American Olean)

Fig. 8-16. Corner strips hide mistakes—and dress up corner. (Courtesy American Olean)

tile will last for years, but occasionally it may be necessary to replace some of the grout if it should become discolored or begin to fall out. Replacing grout is simple. Scrape out old grout with a pointed stick, clean the space with an old toothbrush, and reapply the new grout.

INSTALLING PLASTIC-COATED PANELING

Installing plastic-coated paneling is a simple process, very similar to standard wall paneling except that the panels are attached to the wall with adhesive and the joints between panels fit into moldings that keep the wall waterproof. Moldings are available for inside and outside corners, the top and bottom of panels, and vertical panel joints. Panels are available in 4- by 8-foot sheets.

First, plan the job. Will the plastic paneling run from the floor to the ceiling or only partway? After you have decided this, you can estimate the number of panels necessary for the job. Remember that where ever panels join, you will need the special molding. The most common application of waterproof panels is around the tub, so the following discussion will be for this type of installation.

Inspect the area where the panels will be installed. Panels must be applied over 3/8-inch thick solid backing such as plaster, plywood, or gypsum board (water-resistant). This subwall must be absolutely dry, clean, and sound. Old wallpaper and cracking or peeling paint must be removed. Large holes must be filled with an appropriate type of patching plaster or filler. Remove all soap dishes, railings, faucets, shower heads, etc.

Panels should stand in the room to be paneled at least 24 hours before the job begins. This will give the panels time to become accustomed to the climate of the room.

The tools and materials you will need to install plastic-coated wall paneling are:

Panels and *moldings*
Adhesive and *caulking*
3/16-inch notched trowel and *caulking gun*
Chalk line
Fine-tooth hand saw
Surform plane
Ruler
Hacksaw or *sharp knife* (for cutting moldings)
Hammer and *molding nails*

Fig. 8-17. Grouting the tile joints. (Courtesy American Olean)

Fig. 8-18. Clean off excess grout with cheesecloth and denatured alcohol. (Courtesy American Olean)

Fig. 8-19. A newly tiled bathroom. (Courtesy American Olean)

CAPTIONS FOR FOLLOWING 4-PAGE COLOR SECTION

Plate 1. This monotone painted wall plays a single theme, and variations in the theme arise from a high-styled blend of pearl-white kitchen shutters, a rough-hewn ceiling beam, a mosaic wall tapestry, seamless wall-to-wall flooring, and plain-but-elegant furnishings. (Courtesy Congoleum)

Plate 2. Here's a perfect mixture of design continuity and variety: pastel textured walls are accented by wood paneling and gleaming stainless steel fixtures. (Courtesy NuTone)

Plate 3. Elegant but decorous. The intricate wallpaper suggests the flavor of the 1890s, and this effect is emphasized by antique brass fixtures, dark-wood cabinetry, and a turn-of-the-century mirror. (Courtesy NuTone)

Plate 4. The top photo shows a kitchen freshened by the aura of the South Seas, the result of some well-positioned ferns and vinyl cane-patterned wallcovering. Below, the prim look of gingham. (Courtesy Standard Coated Products)

Mineral spirits — to clean up adhesive

Rags and *drop cloth*

After the surface has been prepared so it is clean, dry, flat, and sound, cover the bathtub with a drop cloth or protective padding to prevent scratching or chipping. Cut the molding that will sit along the rim of the tub, apply a heavy bead of caulk on the rim of the tub, and embed the molding into place. Nail the molding into place through the flange and into the studs in the subwall. Next, find the center of the wall and snap a chalk line through this center, from floor to ceiling (or from tub rim to ceiling). The panels are to be laid from this line *toward* the corners. You may have to cut panels applied in corners. If necessary, subtract up to 1/8 inch from the measurements to compensate for possible out-of-square walls. Trim to fit using a fine-tooth saw and Surform plane. Always cut with the cutting action going into the finished face of the panel.

Fig. 8-20. Checking panel fit. (Courtesy Masonite Corp.)

Set each panel in place to make sure it fits properly (Fig. 8-20). There should be approximately 1/8-inch gap between panels and between panel edges and corners. If a panel is a little out of true, trim the edge with the plane. Mark the top edge of the panel onto the wall. This will be a guide later when you fit the panel.

Install the inside corner moldings with hammer and nails, making sure that the nailheads are set just below the surface of the molding. Before the panels can be attached to the wall, two things must take place: The moldings must be half filled with caulking, and adhesive must be applied to the surface of the wall.

Apply the caulking to the inside of the moldings with a caulking gun. The panels will later be set into the moldings. After the panels have all been cut and dry fitted to the wall, you can begin applying the adhesive to the surface of the subwall with the notched trowel. Spread the adhesive with one motion of the notched trowel. Retroweling causes the adhesive to stiffen and considerably shortens the open time.

Put the above-tub panel in place on the wall, forcing it down into the tub molding and into the corner. Force the panel down until the pencil line along the top of the panel is visible. Cut one length of edge molding to fit the top of the panel. Place caulking into the molding and slip the molding onto the top of the panel. It may be necessary to pull the panel slightly away from the wall to force the edge molding over the panel. After the edge molding has been put on, the entire panel may be permanently bonded to the wall by pressing over the entire face of the panel. Install other corner panels in the same fashion and finish the edges with edge moldings. Careful measurements will be necessary for the holes of plumbing fixtures and accessories. Hole location can be simplified with the use of a cardboard template. Holes are cut with a keyhole saw or circle cutter.

Make certain all panels are well bonded. Remove excess adhesive with a soft cloth and mineral spirits; remove the caulking with a soft cloth and water. Plastic-coated wall panels should be allowed to set for 24 hours before use.

Care and cleaning of plastic-coated waterproof wall panels is simple. Use a mild detergent or soap and water for cleaning most soil. Soap residue and water spots can usually be wiped off with a damp rag. All manufacturers agree that you should never use any type of abrasive cleanser on the panels. Nor should you apply adhesive tape or stickers.

Chapter 9
Wood for Your Walls

Before prefinished paneling came onto the home decorating scene, walls were covered with wooden boards and planks from such trees as oak, cherry, maple, teak, rosewood, and ebony. Soon large trees became scarce, and as a result the cost of covering interior walls with *natural* paneling became prohibitive for all except the very wealthy.

Today, covering an interior wall with natural wood is more expensive than covering the same wall with prefinished paneling. But for a few dollars and more time per foot, you can transform interior walls into unique works of art. Walls that will be extensions of your lifestyle and personality.

Some of the contemporary natural wood wall coverings are cedar shingles, hand-split cedar shakes, redwood boards, knotty pine boards, rough-sawn boards, barn siding (either recycled or manufactured), and flooring. The possibilities are boundless. Once you opt for natural wood wall coverings, let your pocketbook and the amount of available time be your guide. With a little imagination and a few simple hand tools, you can impart your personal mark of creativity to the walls that surround you (Fig. 9-1).

MAKING LUMBER

Let's look at how lumber is milled. After a tree has been cut and brought to the mill, it is run through the saw four times. These initial passes through the mill square off the log lengthwise. The four cuts result in a square timber—length and width depending on the size of the original log—and four boards, rough sawn on one side, with the bark on the other side. The four boards are called slab wood, a waste product to be burned or thrown away.

Next, the timber is cut into boards or dimensional lumber— 2 × 4s, for example. At smaller mills all cuts are done with a blade that is for ripping. The boards and dimensional lumber are rough sawn. You can buy lumber in the rough-sawn stage for considerably less than dressed lumber. Rough lumber has been sawed, edged, and trimmed but has not been surfaced.

Dressing lumber is generally the next step at a mill. Dressed lumber has been surfaced on one or more sides to remove saw marks and surface blemishes. The most common dressed lumber is surfaced on all sides (S4S). Most of the boards for sale at your local lumberyard are dressed; they are smooth on all sides and have square edges.

A mill may perform several other operations to lumber, depending on the machinery, manpower and market. Lumber that is further processed is commonly referred to as "worked." Worked lumber can be tongue and grooved (T & G), shiplapped, beveled, channeled, or patterned.

Obviously the more work done to a piece of lumber the higher the price. Another operation that is often done to lumber is kiln drying. Kiln-dried lumber is, in effect, baked to remove moisture from the wood. This operation is necessary for any boards that will be used inside the home. Lumber that has not been kiln dried is referred to as green lumber and will shrink, depending on the type of wood, as much as 30% after installation in the relatively dry interior of the home.

THE VARIETY OF WOOD WALL COVERINGS

Ten years ago, shingles and shakes were used solely for exterior surfaces. Now, however, the building industry has found new applications inside the home.

Interior designers, architects, builders and style conscious homeowners are switching to the natural ruggedness and warmth of shingles and shakes. Carefree maintenance with the look of high fashion is possible with fancy-cut shingles. The same

Fig. 9-1. Red cedar hand-split shakes can give a room a touch of the country, a bit of rustic charm. (Courtesy Red Cedar Shingle & Hand-Split Shake Bureau)

121

maintenance—almost none—comes with the rugged looking hand-split shake. Their rough texture is suggestive of mountains and wilderness. Some homeowners like the smoother shingle, some the more aggressive shake. But all seem to agree that both offer an intriguing approach to room decoration.

Inside the home, the stringent exposure rules common to exterior applications do not apply. Cedar shingles and shakes may be laid at any exposure, staggered at will, used sideways or, if desired, upside down. Furthermore, any grade or type of shingle may be used.

In the last few years, some innovative designers have used wood flooring materials to cover interior walls. The result is unusual and distinctive. Finish flooring—both hardwood and softwood— is commonly tongue and grooved and available in a variety of widths, lengths, and thicknesses. Lengths of finish flooring can be attached to interior wall surfaces with nails or adhesive, horizontally, vertically, or diagonally.

Finish flooring is available in hardwoods and softwoods. Hardwoods most commonly used for flooring are red and white oak, beech, maple, and pecan. Hardwood flooring is tough but expensive. However, if you are only covering one wall, to accent a living room for example, the attractive grain patterns of the hardwoods will help to create a very special look.

Softwood finish flooring is usually made from southern pine, Douglas fir, redwood, and western hemlock. These coniferous woods are much softer and must be protected when used on floors. But when used on interior walls, softwood finish flooring needs little protection. A coat of wax or polyurethane will let the natural beauty of softwood show and shield against nicks and grime.

Both hardwood and softwood finish flooring are available in prefinished and unfinished grades—and a variety of colors and grain patterns. Some homeowners achieve unique walls by mixing grains and colors.

If your decorating plans are limited by a tight budget, you can still achieve the custom look for your walls by using recycled materials. There are several ways that you can cover any wall in your home for next to nothing, providing you have some time and a strong desire to create distinctive looking interior walls. Old barn siding, solid wall paneling from an old house, mill ends, even crating and pallets…whatever you can get your hands on can turn your wall into something exciting.

Recycling is not for everyone. Obviously, an investment of many hours is needed to find, condition, and install recycled wall coverings. But salvaging old wood does not necessarily mean rescuing junk. Around 50 to 60 years ago, America underwent a period known as the Golden Oak Era. At this time the houses of the newly rich were built. These showplaces were often paneled in quartered oak. A quarter-sawed plank of full breadth is one which has one edge at the center of the tree and the other just under the bark. The effect is striking, to say the least. Golden oak was the name for a high-gloss varnish that was applied to the finished walls. Today it is nearly impossible to buy quarter oak paneling. You have to retrieve it from old, dilapidated houses built in the Goden Oak Era.

Today many old houses are filled with other rich woods. Besides oak, interior walls of the finer houses were covered with walnut, chestnut, maple, teak, you name it. Wall paneling like this is just not available anymore, except through recycling.

Old barn siding has risen to popularity over the past 10 years. There is something spiritual about boards that have been weathered by time. The softer grain of the wood gets worn away by the elements, and what is left gets bleached by the sun. Old barn siding looks rugged at first glance, but as you get closer, a natural, distinctive beauty becomes apparent.

If there are any old, deserted farms in your area, or if you know that an old barn will be torn down, ask the owner if you can have some of the old siding. In many cases the owner will be glad to have someone take the lumber away.

Recycling barn siding takes time. You have to pull out nails and sort through a lot of useless boards. But with a small amount of conscientious work, you will be able to add real character to the walls of your home.

In my area (upstate New York), barn siding is so popular with decorators and builders that there are precious few old barns around. As a result, there are a few companies selling manufactured barn siding through lumberyards. This "old" barn siding resembles the real thing—and you don't have to hunt for it. Available in either 8- or 10-foot lengths, with widths of 4, 6, 8, and 10 inches. Manufactured barn siding sells for around $1 for an 8-foot 1 × 6 (Fig. 9-2).

Fig. 9-2. Manufactured "barn siding." (Courtesy Barclay Industries, Inc.)

Homeowners have been known to recycle shipping crates or pallets, which are made from rough-sawn softwood planks. Usually the planks have to be sanded down before they are applied to walls.

Tools for recycling crates and pallets, as well as barn siding or old walls, are: a wrecking bar, crow bar, hammer, and gloves. Any nails, screws, staples, or other fasteners should be removed before you begin to work with any recycled lumber.

If there is a lumber mill in your area, you may be able to obtain rough-sawn lumber, which makes an interesting interior wall covering. In fact, one type of rough-sawn lumber can usually be had for the asking: slab lumber. Slab wood ranges in thickness from 1 to around 2 inches. If you have access to slab lumber, consider using it to refinish an interior wall in your home. There are two effects that you can achieve using slab wood: the rough-sawn board look or the exposed-bark look. It is simply a matter of which side of the slab you want showing in your home. However, a small amount of work will be necessary to transform the slabs in boards because you must square off the edges. This is no problem because one side of the slab has been sawn and is flat. Simply mark the edges, using a chalk line or long straightedge, then cut the edges off the slab using a table or hand-held circular saw. You will end up with boards that have a rough-sawn face, square straight edges, and a back with the bark still on.

You can then attach the reworked slab lumber to an interior wall. Nail with the rough-sawn face showing or, for a rustic log cabin look, with the bark side showing.

Remember though that slab lumber is green; that is, it's unseasoned. So unless it has been air or kiln dried before it's attached to interior walls, it will shrink. To help eliminate shrinkage, you should store the worked slab wood in a dry place for a minimum of 3 months. Stack it with spacers between the boards to permit air circulation.

SURFACE PREPARATION

No matter what kind of wood wall covering you use to redecorate your walls, there is generally some type of surface preparation involved. Surface preparation will usually not be extensive, but walls should be flat and free from falling plaster. Holes should be filled, of course, and insulation should be checked (where possible) to help reduce heat loss. Moldings around windows and doors should be removed and replaced after the new wall covering has been attached.

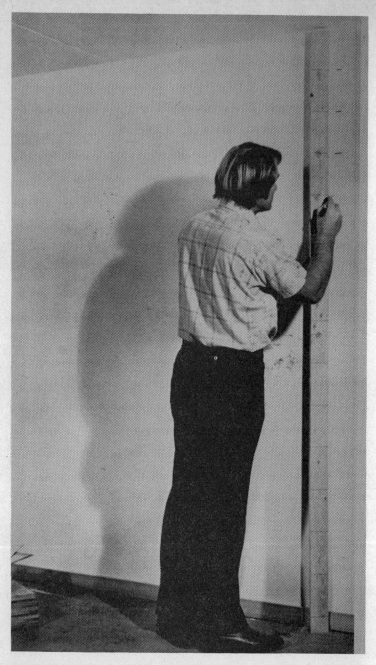

Fig. 9-3. Transfer the markings from the batten to the wall. (Courtesy Red Cedar Shingle & Hand-Split Shake Bureau)

ATTACHING SHINGLES TO YOUR WALLS

Shingles are attached in horizontal courses (rows), with each course (except the first one) overlapping an adjacent course below. So the first step is to mark where the courses will go, making sure that each shingle will have the same exposure. To do this, calculate the number of courses to be attached by dividing the height of the wall (minus the height of the baseboard, if any) by the width of the desired exposure. Mark the position of each course on a batten, and transfer the markings to the walls (Fig. 9-3). Align furring strips (1 × 2s) with the markings and nail them into place, driving the nails into the wall studs (Fig. 9-4). The shingles are nailed to the furring strips.

The first course of shingles is attached near the floor. You will notice in Fig. 9-5 that a spacer is used to keep the bottom edges of the shingles approximately 2 inches off the floor.

The first course of shingles should be a double course. There are unavoidable spaces between attached shingles, so by making the first course double, any gaps will show shingle, not bare wall. Because all other courses overlap preceding courses, double coursing is only necessary on the first row.

Succeeding courses are attached to the furring strips until the entire wall has been covered. Tack a straightedge to the wall to keep each course properly aligned (Fig. 9-6). Use a level to make sure that straightedge is true. Remember that each course should cover the nailheads of preceding courses.

Overlap shingles at outside corners, alternately exposing one edge and then another. Then plane the extending edges flush (Fig. 9-7). When planing the edges of shingles, always push the plane from the thicker, bottom edge toward the thinner, top edge. Planing from the thick to the thin edge of the shingle will minimize splitting.

The last course of shingles, at the ceiling, should be cut to insure a good fit and straight edges. First, measure the distance between the last course and the ceiling, keeping in mind the exposure spacing used throughout the rest of the wall. Measure up from the thick edge of a shingle and cut the shingle with a handsaw to the required length (Fig. 9-8). Discard the top section. A fine-toothed saw should be used for all cuts; this will minimize split or ragged edges. Place the cut shingle in position at the top of the wall and check for proper fit. The top edge should be flush with the ceiling and the bottom edge should cover the preceding course's nailheads. If

Fig. 9-4. Fasten 1- by 2-inch battens to the wall. (Courtesy Red Cedar Shingle and Hand-Split Shake Bureau)

Fig. 9-5. Start with a double course at the bottom of the wall. (Courtesy Red Cedar Shingle and Hand-Split Shake Bureau)

Fig. 9-6. Continue with single courses to the top of the wall. (Courtesy Red Cedar Shingle and Hand-Split Shake Bureau)

Fig. 9-7. Alternately overlap the shingles on the outside corner to produce an interlaced effect. (Courtesy Red Cedar Shingle and Hand-Split Shake Bureau)

Fig. 9-8. Cut the shingles with a handsaw. (Courtesy Red Cedar Shingle and Hand-Split Shake Bureau)

you are satisfied with the fit, use this shingle as a guide for cutting the rest of the shingles needed to complete the wall. The last course of shingles is then nailed into place as in Fig. 9-9.

Of course, you can also attach shingles with an adhesive, in which case furring strips won't be necessary.

Wood shingles or hand-split shakes can be left in their natural state or can be sealed with thinned linseed oil. Lacquer, varnish, polyurethane, or stain wax will help to bring out and preserve the natural beauty of shingles or shakes. Or you can paint or stain them any color; semi-transparent stain will allow the wood's natural beauty to show through. The easiest and most efficient way to paint

Fig. 9-9. Glue and nail the last course in place. (Courtesy Red Cedar Shingle and Hand-Split Shake Bureau)

Fig. 9-10. The shingles can be sealed with wax-based sealer, stain, or paint. (Courtesy Red Cedar Shingle and Hand-Split Shake Bureau)

134

or stain shingles or shakes is with a 3- or 4-inch-wide paint brush, as in Fig. 9-10.

In just a few hours an average size interior wall can be covered with shingles. The cost of covering an interior wall will vary with the size of the wall and the exposure, but because the shingles need not battle the elements, the less expensive grades can be used. A no. 4 grade cedar shingle, for example, is a utility grade because of its high incidence of knots. Though its exterior use is limited to undercoursing, inside the home this shingle is just right for accent walls. Price no. 4 grade or undercoursing shingles at your local lumberyard. The cost of covering a wall in your home may be well within your budget. And you will be pleased with the decorator's touch they will add to your walls.

COVERING WALLS WITH DRESSED OR WORKED LUMBER

If you are covering the interior walls in your home with dressed or worked lumber, very little surface preparation is necessary. Dressed lumber can be tongue and groove, shiplap, beveled, or rabbeted bevel. Dressed lumber and worked lumber are available in lengths of 8 feet and longer and can be attached to your walls horizontally, vertically, or at angles. Conventional methods of attachment, nailing or adhesive, are best for professional looking results.

Bevel, rabbeted, and shiplap dressed lumber is most commonly attached horizontally. The boards are nailed either directly to the studs or through the existing wall covering into the studs.

Nails should be long enough to penentrate into the studs, at least 1 1/2 inches long. Use stainless steel, aluminum, or high-quality hotdipped galvanized nails to hold the boards to interior walls. Other types of nails—common iron and some galvanized nails for example—will rust if exposed to moisture and will stain the boards.

Figure 9-11 illustrates various nailing methods used to attach lumber to walls. Always use a nailset to sink nails flush with the surface.

ATTACHING FINISH FLOORING TO WALLS

Finish flooring may be attached to the wall surface with adhesive. But plywood sheeting must first be attached to the surface of the wall. The surfaces should be flat and free of dirt to insure a strong bond.

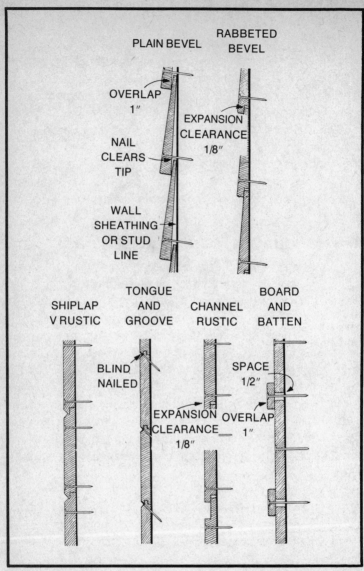

PLAIN BEVEL

RABBETED BEVEL

OVERLAP 1"

EXPANSION CLEARANCE 1/8"

NAIL CLEARS TIP

WALL SHEATHING OR STUD LINE

SHIPLAP V RUSTIC

TONGUE AND GROOVE

CHANNEL RUSTIC

BOARD AND BATTEN

BLIND NAILED

SPACE 1/2"

EXPANSION CLEARANCE 1/8"

OVERLAP 1"

Fig. 9-11. Suggested nailing methods. (Courtesy California Redwood Assoc.)

Use a good paneling adhesive. Begin attaching the finish flooring by nailing the first course at the bottom of the wall. If you are
attaching hardwood flooring, it may be necessary to drill the nail
holes first. After the first course has been attached, cover a section
of the wall with panel adhesive. Spread adhesive with a notched

trowel along the entire horizontal length of the wall, covering a strip about 2 feet wide.

Place each flooring board on the surface of the wall and interlock it with the preceding board. Tap each piece into place with a block and hammer. This will insure that solid contact has been made with the wall and the previous course. Continue in this fashion until the entire wall has been covered with the flooring.

The last course of flooring may have to be cut for a tight fit. The last course should be face nailed. Face nail with either finishing nails (countersunk) or common nails. If common nails are used, molding should be installed to conceal the heads.

Occasionally, when attaching finish flooring to an interior wall with adhesive, it may be necessary to nail a few stubborn pieces so they will lie flat. In fact, it makes good sense to nail every *fifth* course of flooring to keep the joints tight. Nail in the same fashion as you would any tongue-and-groove board.

An interesting effect can be achieved by covering your interior walls with tongue-and-grooved redwood boards or planks, 6- to 8-inch widths. Begin by buying the required number of boards and cutting them all to the required wall height. Next, stack them in the room so you can sort them, for the best effect, according to color and grain pattern (Fig. 9-12).

Panel adhesive is applied to the back of each board with the aid of a caulking gun (Fig. 9-13). Each board is then set vertically against the wall and interlocked with the preceding board (Fig. 9-14). A block of wood can be used to tap the boards tightly together (Fig. 9-15). If you are planning to use molding at the top and bottom of the wall, you can drive two nails at both the top and bottom of each board. Nails should be long enough to penetrate through the board, the wall covering, and the sole or top plate. Drive the nails into the top and bottom of each board at a level that will be covered by molding.

Holes for electrical outlets and heating ducts can be cut with a hand-held jig saw. Measure and cut carefully to insure that the hole will be covered with electrical strike plates or heat registers (Fig. 9-16).

Boards can be attached under windows just as they are elsewhere, but first a horizontal board, of narrower width, should be attached under the window sill (Fig. 9-17). The vertical boards can

Fig. 9-12. Stack the boards, then sort them before applying to the walls. (Courtesy California Redwood Assoc.)

Fig. 9-13. Caulk the boards with panel adhesive. (Courtesy California Redwood Assoc.)

Fig. 9-14. Lay the boards against the wall and interlock them. (Courtesy California Redwood Assoc.)

Fig. 9-15. Tap the boards together. (Courtesy California Redwood Assoc.)

Fig. 9-16. Cut the boards to make room for strike plates and registers. (Courtesy California Redwood Assoc.)

Fig. 9-17. Attach a board under the window sill. (Courtesy California Redwood Assoc.)

Fig. 9-18. Butt vertical boards against the horizontal piece. (Courtesy California Redwood Assoc.)

then be attached to the wall with adhesive. The top edge of the boards should butt against the horizontal strip (Fig. 9-18).

The walls are finished off with molding and attached to the top and bottom of the wall (Fig. 9-9). Moldings will also be needed around door and window openings.

Redwood boards can be left natural, oiled, varnished, or coated with polyurethane. Without a finish, redwood indoors will change from red to a mellow, brownish red. It will take several years for this change in color, however.

Consider applying some type of clear sealer. This will help to retard the color change and offer some protection against stains, marks, and nicks.

If you are attaching redwood boards in high-moisture areas, such as the bathroom or kitchen, some type of sealer should be applied. Several coats of clear varnish, lacquer, or polyurethane are the best protection against spots or stains caused by water. Flat finishes are the most natural looking, but a glossy finish is easier to wipe clean.

ATTACHING SLAB WOOD TO YOUR WALLS

Slab wood that has been edge squared and properly dried can be attached in several ways. One style of slab wood wall covering is called board and batten. To achieve this look, 8-, 10-, or 12-inch-wide boards are nailed upright (bark side down) to the wall, spaced 1 inch apart. Use a level to plumb the boards, then facenail them. Drive nails at the top, bottom, and 1 inch in from the edges, with 2-foot spacing. After the entire wall has been covered with the boards, facenail the battens between the boards. Nails should be long enough to pass through the batten and into the wall covering underneath. The board-and-batten style is ideal for semi-green boards because any shrinkage of the boards is usually concealed by the battens. Old barn siding looks good when attached to interior walls in the board-and-batten style.

Slab wood can also be attached to interior walls with the bark side facing out. Nail the fully dried boards horizontally on the surface of the wall. Facenail 1 inch up from the bottom and 1 inch down from the top of each board and into the wall studs. Use long shanked nails to insure a strong attachment to the surface of the wall. If, as the boards acclimate themselves to the relative humidity of the room,

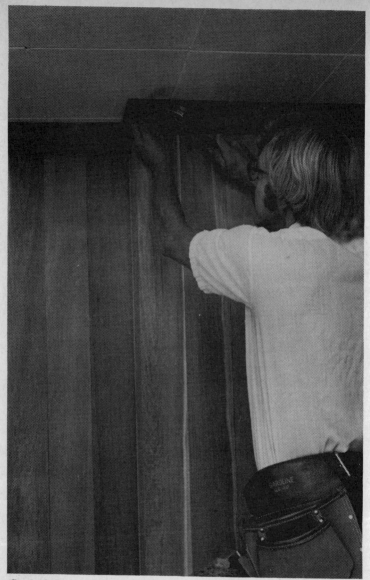

Fig. 9-19. Nail molding to the top and bottom of the wall. (Courtesy California Redwood Assoc.)

spaces widen between the boards, you can fill them with white caulking. Another, more time consuming treatment for spaces between the boards is to apply a coat of black paint, with a small brush, between the boards.

Chapter 10
Wallpaper

There are literally hundreds of wallpaper styles, colors, and textures to choose from. From flower prints, to bold stripes, to quiet checks, to shiny foils, there is a wallpaper that is just what you need to make your walls look like an interior decorator's masterpiece.

Painted walls need repainting every 2 or 3 years to keep them looking fresh. But good quality wallpaper should last at least twice as long. In high-traffic high-moisture areas (playrooms, bathrooms, kitchens, etc.), use vinyl wallpaper. Vinyl will resist destruction and can be wiped clean with a damp cloth.

SOME THINGS TO REMEMBER

When you redecorate with wallpaper, keep the following in mind:

1. Keep your redecorating simple.
2. Your carpeting, furnishings, and wall coverings are interrelated. They should be blended and balanced with taste.
3. Color affects our emotions. Yellow, pink, red, and orange suggest lightness and mirth. Darker colors suggest warmth and more solemn moods. So choose wallpaper colors that will help to create the atmosphere that suits you best.
4. Increase the effectiveness of wallpaper by painting the trim and moldings. Paint these a color that will match the

background color of the wallpaper. Paint *before* you hang the new wallpaper.

TYPES OF WALLPAPER

An understanding of the following types of wallpaper will help you choose the type best suited for your needs:

Strippable wallpaper A double-strength synthetic material that is amazingly strong, wet or dry. It's engineered to help you avoid the rip and tear associated with handling of ordinary wet wallpaper and to aid in easy removal when redecorating. Complete strips can be pulled from the wall in seconds.

Nonstrippable wallpaper The pattern is printed on a paper stock, or metal foil sheeting is laminated to a paper stock. Nonstrippable wallpaper requires careful handling when hanging. To remove this type of wallcovering, you must scrape or steam it off. A messy, time-consuming task at best.

Fabric-backed vinyl wallpaper Woven cloth backing identifies this type of wallcovering. The quality of the vinyl film determines whether this wallcovering is washable or scrubbable. All fabric-backed vinyl wallpaper is strippable. A popular example of this type of wallcovering is the high-gloss type.

Prepasted wallpaper A dry, water-activated adhesive is applied to the back of this wallcovering at the factory. Simply cut the desired length of strip from the roll, submerge in water (according to instructions), and the adhesive will become activated. Pull the paper from the water and hang. (Some manufacturers suggest that you wait a few minutes before hanging the wet paper.) Prepasted wallpaper eliminates the need to mix and apply adhesive to the wallpaper back.

Flock wallpaper A velour-like surface is put on this wallpaper during production by adhesion of minute rayon fibers to the base material. The surface is usually completely washable with soap and water. Vacuuming may be necessary to keep this type of wallcovering looking fresh.

Pretrimmed wallpaper Strips of this wallpaper are cut to common lengths at the factory, eliminating the need for time-consuming hand trimming. Pretrimming is a real aid to matching seams and will enable you to paper a wall quicker than with a conventional roll of paper. Standard lengths are 8, 10, and 12 feet.

Wallpaper squares A fairly new concept in wallpaper. Available as prepasted, vinyl coated and dry-strippable. Very simple for single wall application, no mess and no special tools are required.

MATERIAL AND TOOLS

Table 10-1 will help you estimate the number of single rolls of wallpaper you will need to cover an average-sized room. You must first measure the length and width of the room, then the ceiling height. Subtract one single roll for every two regular-sized openings (i.e., windows and doors).

Tools necessary for just about any paperhanging job are:

Stepladder

Yardstick

Scissors

Razor knife—with plenty of single-edged blades

Seam roller—for pressing and setting seams

Wallscraper—at least 4 inches wide for trimming with knife

Plumb line—use a carpenter's chalk line or make one

Smoothing brush—short nap for vinyl; long nap for most other wallpaper

Sponge and *bucket*

Sandpaper and *sanding block*—for surface preparation

Drop cloths—or plenty of newspaper for protecting carpets and floors

Screwdriver, hammer, and *nailset*—for removing switch plates and tapping nails that protrude

Workingtable—It's easier to work on a raised surface than the floor. Table should be covered with brown paper; newspaper might discolor or smear wallpaper.

Watertray—for wetting prepasted wallpaper

Patching plaster or *Spackle*—for surface preparation

Paste brush, bucket, and *adhesive* for unpasted wallpaper

Table 10-1. Wallpaper Estimating Table.

Size of Room	For 8-foot ceiling	For 9-foot ceiling	For 10-foot ceiling
8×10	9	10	11
10×10	10	11	13
10×12	11	12	14
10×14	12	14	15
12×12	12	14	15
12×14	13	15	16
12×16	14	16	17
12×18	15	17	19
12×20	16	18	20
14×14	14	16	17
14×16	15	17	19
14×18	16	18	20
14×20	17	19	21
14×22	18	20	22
16×16	16	18	20
16×18	17	19	21
16×20	18	20	22
16×22	19	21	23
16×24	20	22	25
18×18	18	20	22
18×20	19	21	23
18×22	20	22	25
18×24	21	23	26

Size—if recommended for surface preparation

Vinyl-to-vinyl adhesive—for overlapping seams and special surfaces

The most important tools are the simple ones; razor knife and the wallscraper will probably get the most use. Change the blade in the knife often, and it will cut cleanly.

SURFACE PREPARATION

Most interior walls are covered with either plaster or dry wallboard (gypsum panels), so unless your walls are in really terrible shape (i.e., falling or missing plaster, holes, etc.), surface preparation will be easy.

The first thing to do is to remove all pictures, picture hooks, shelves, brackets, lighting fixtures, switch plates, and anything else attached to the wall (Fig. 10-1). Next, fill nail holes and cracks with Spackle or painter's plaster. Let dry; sand smooth. Countersink nailheads. If the wall has been previously painted, check the condition of the paint and remove any peeling or loose paint. Sand the edges of any area where the paint has been removed. If mildew is present, wash the affected area with a solution of three parts water and one part liquid bleach. Scrub the area with a medium soft brush, keeping the surface wet until the stain is bleached out. Rinse with clear water and let dry.

Usually old wallpaper should be removed. Unfortunately, most older houses have wallpaper that is not strippable, so it will require a fair amount of work to remove it. There are two ways of removing nonstrippable wallpaper: the dry method and the wet method.

The dry method involves the use of special scrapers and lots of elbow grease. After all the old paper has been removed, the residue is wiped off with steel wool and warm water.

The wet method entails the use of a solution of warm water and vinegar or a commercial wallpaper stripper. Begin by soaking the entire wall with the stripping solution; let set for 20 minutes. Then

Fig. 10-1. Remove everything attached to the walls. (Courtesy Imperial Wallcoverings)

Fig. 10-2. Imperial Wall Cover can be used to line concrete, cement block, grooved paneling, or old plaster.

resoak one section at a time and remove the wallpaper with a hand scraper. If the solution does not penetrate, score the face of the paper with your scraper or coarse sandpaper and reapply the stripping solution. Protect your floors with a drop cloth or plenty of newspaper. Removing old wallpaper is a messy job, but it must be done unless the existing wallpaper is firmly fastened to the walls.

If the existing wallpaper is in good enough shape to remain on the wall, check it over for air bubbles. Slice an X across the face of any bubbles and glue down the loose cut edges. The surface of existing wallpaper should be as smooth as possible. Level any uneven places with Spackle; let dry and sand smooth.

It is often necessary to prime bare walls before hanging wallpaper. Primer should be applied to new walls and any area that has been Spackled. A coat of primer over mildewed areas (after they have been cleaned) will do a lot to prevent the area from becoming mildewed again. If you are uncertain as to the quality of the paint on existing walls, give them a coat of oil-base primer sealer. If wallboard is to be covered with lightweight or transparent wallpaper, the wallboard should be primed to prevent "show through."

Size serves as a base for wallpaper. It can usually be brushed, rolled, or sponged on the wall. Size acts as a sealer that separates the old wall surface from the new wallpaper. The size you use depends on the kind of wallpaper you plan to hang. Follow manufacturer's instructions.

If you are applying wallpaper over concrete, cinder block, cement block, grooved paneling, or old plaster, you might consider first covering the walls with Imperial Wall Cover (Fig. 10-2). Imperial makes it unnecessary to fill mortar joints or minor cracks and recesses. After the Imperial has dried to the surface, wallpaper is applied directly to it (Fig. 10-3).

Moldings around windows and doors should be painted *before* wallpapering. Always sand glossy surfaces before painting. You might consider painting the ceiling in the room to be wallpapered; this should be done before the actual hanging begins. Let any painting job dry for at least 24 hours before you begin hanging wallpaper.

HANGING THE WALLPAPER

It is a good idea to unroll each roll of wallpaper to inspect for defects before you begin the job. Inspecting each roll will not only prevent any problems when you are actually hanging but will also make the wallpaper easier to work with (Fig. 10-4).

After surface preparation has been completed, draw a straight line from ceiling to floor. Make sure that the line is true. This line will

Fig. 10-3. Wallpaper can be applied directly over the Imperial Wall Cover.

be your guide and will insure that the first strip of wallpaper will hang straight. If you don't have a yardstick, snap the line onto the wall with a chalk line. It's best to position the line near a window or door. Measure out from the door or window molding approximately the width of a strip of wallpaper, less 1 inch. That is, if the wall paper is

27 inches, measure out 26 inches. Mark where the line is to go. To insure that the line is plumb, tack a plumb line to your mark where the wall meets the ceiling. Let the string (and weight) hang to just above the floor (Fig. 10-5). When the string stops swinging, mark its position against the wall. Then draw (or snap) your line (Fig. 10-6).

Assuming that you are not using pretrimmed wallpaper, you will have to measure the height of your wall and cut strips to that length. Add about 8 inches to your wall height, 4 inches on both the top and the bottom.

Next, if you are using prepasted wallpaper, wet a strip; if you are using conventional wallpaper, apply adhesive. One simple way to

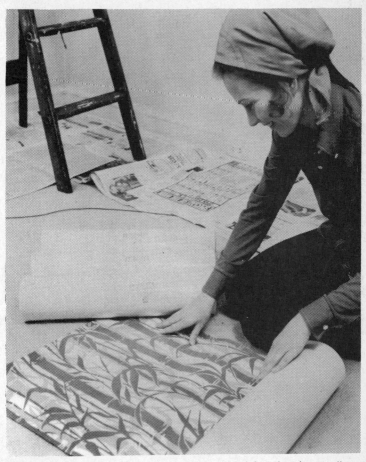

Fig. 10-4. Before wallpapering, inspect each roll for defects in color or pattern. (Courtesy Sunworthy)

Fig. 10-5. Make a straight line from ceiling to floor with plumb line. (Courtesy Imperial Wallcoverings)

wet prepasted wallpaper is to fill a water tray with lukewarm water (Fig. 10-7). Place this tray on the floor in front of the marked wall section. (Specially designed water trays are available for just this purpose.) Loosely reroll the first strip from bottom to top with pattern side in, paste side out. Submerge the rolled strip in water for the length of time specified by the wallpaper manufacturer.

When the first strip has soaked for the required time, pull it slowly out of the water tray, climb your ladder, and carry the top of the strip to the ceiling line. Place the wet strip on the wall so that it overlaps at the ceiling about 4 inches. Line up one edge of the strip with the marked plumb line and let the other edge overlap the corner of the wall or window (Fig. 10-8).

Wipe the upper section of the strip (at the ceiling line) with a smoothing brush or sponge. Work down the wall, aligning the edge of the strip with the chalk line, brushing out air bubbles (Fig. 10-9). Brush down and toward the sides. Continue down the wall in this fashion until you have come to the floor. The wallpaper should extend below the bottom of the wall about 4 inches. Brush the entire strip and wipe off any paste that may have gotten on the face of the strip. Make sure that the edges are securely fastened to the wall by rebrushing the entire strip.

After the first strip has been attached to the wall, trim off the excess wallpaper. The paper should extend approximately 4 inches above and below the wall, and these are the areas that must be trimmed. Figure 10-10 shows a razor knife and edge guide being used to trim off the excess wallpaper. An edge guide is pressed against the wall and down towards the baseboard. Then a razor knife is used to cut the wallpaper along the bottom of the guide.

Hang the second strip on the wall so its pattern mates with that of the first strip. Seams should be butted together without overlapping. To avoid stretching the wallpaper, use the palms of your hands and work at the center of the strip as much as possible when positioning each strip.

Fig. 10-6. Use a ruler and pencil to make the line. (Courtesy Sunworthy)

Fig. 10-7. Soak prepasted wallpaper to activate the adhesive. (Courtesy Sun-worthy)

When hanging nonpatterned or textured wallcoverings (burlap, cork, etc.), it is advisable to reverse each strip as the wallcovering is hung. When this type of wallcovering is printed, the color tends to be heavier or darker on one edge. By reversing each strip, dark edges will butt against dark edges, and light edges will butt against light edges.

After each strip has been hung it should be rinsed entirely with a wet sponge to remove any paste on the surface. Be sure to thoroughly rinse ceilings and moldings to remove any excess paste. Use clean water for rinsing. Change rinse water after hanging two or three strips.

It is always best to use one entire roll of paper before using the next. Colors and pattern may vary slightly between rolls. After each wall has been completed, use a seam roller to roll seams with firm but not excessive pressure. Keep the seam roller clean and free of paste. Do not roll the seams of flocked or embossed paper: the pressure from the roller may crush the delicate velour-like finish. Apply even pressure with a soft, dry cloth to the seams of flocked wallpaper.

When you come to an electrical outlet or switch, turn off the current if possible to avoid electrical shock. (Great care must be taken in the installation of foil wallpaper so that it does not come in contact with live electrical wiring.) Remove the fixture cover. Hang the wallpaper right over the fixture. With a single-edge razor blade,

Fig. 10-8. Use the plumb line as a guide. (Courtesy Sunworthy)

Fig. 10-9. Brush out air bubbles with a sponge. (Courtesy Sunworthy)

cut away the paper covering the fixture. Replace the fixture cover after you have made the cuts.

Don't try to precut wallpaper to fit around doors and windows. This never works. Hang the wallpaper right over the edge of the opening. With a pair of scissors, trim off as much of the excess as possible; make diagonal cuts at the corners with a razor knife. Using an edge guide and razor knife, trim off the excess paper all around the window or door frame (Fig. 10-11). Fireplaces and heat registers are treated in the same manner.

A single strip of wallpaper must be used to cover each inside corner. First fit the strip into the corner, pressing it against only one

Fig. 10-10. Trim off excess paper with an edge guide and knife. (Courtesy Imperial Wallcoverings)

wall, aligning its edge against the preceding strip. Mark the position of its other edge. Cut off the unpressed side of the strip, 1/2 inch from the corner. Then measure from the corner to within 1/2 inch of the edge mark; mark this distance on the wall (Fig. 10-12). Secure

Fig. 10-11. Trim the paper around windows. (Courtesy Imperial Wallcoverings)

Fig. 10-12. Mark the other wall with a pencil. (Courtesy Sunworthy)

the 1/2-inch flap of unpressed wallpaper with special adhesive (called seam adhesive). Then hang the remainder of the strip, butting it into the corner over the flap, smoothing out wrinkles (Fig. 10-13). Trim off excess paper at the ceiling line.

This kind of overlapping is necessary on all inside corners, on some outside corners, and on ceiling lines when the ceiling will be papered.

Usually the most practical way to wallpaper an outside corner is to wrap a strip around the corner. Since no ceiling or corner is exactly straight, you may have to tolerate a slight pattern drop or slant at the ceiling line when butting the next strip against the corner strip. For this reason, when you have to wrap wallpaper around an outside corner, start on the longer wall. This way any pattern drop at the ceiling line caused by an imperfect corner will be on the shorter wall and thus less conspicuous.

When you are going to cover only one wall of an outside corner, hang the wallpaper within 1/4 inch of the corner to eliminate fraying or peeling of the paper.

To cover a ceiling, follow the same procedure as for walls. Let the ceiling strips overlap 1/4 to 1/2 inch onto the walls. The overlap can then be either cut off or covered when the walls are wallpapered. Work clockwise rather than lengthwise. If you are planning to wallpaper both ceiling and walls, cover the ceiling first.

Fig. 10-13. Lap the remainder of the strip into the corner. (Courtesy Sunworthy)

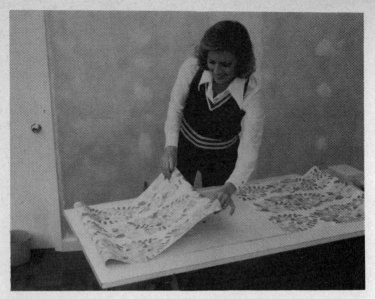

Fig. 10-14. Fold each strip, end to end. (Courtesy Imperial Wallcoverings)

Usually it takes two people to wallpaper a ceiling because it takes two to smooth the strips to the ceiling; both ends of the strip must be smoothed at the same time. The sweep of a long handled broom will help you get the wallpaper up; once there, you can slide it into position.

Conventional wallpaper is hung in the same way as prepasted wallpaper. However, pasting conventional strips is easier if you have a long worktable. Apply suitable adhesive to the back of each strip with a paste brush. Begin applying the adhesive at the top of the strip and work down the strip until it is evenly covered. Consider using a paint roller and tray to apply the adhesive to the back of the paper. The paste will go on much quicker and the roller will help to spread it evenly.

Fold each strip loosely, paste to paste, along the center (Fig. 10-14). Do not crease. It is possible to paste up several strips at a time; adhesive usually takes 15 to 20 minutes to set. If, as you begin to hang, you notice that the paste has dried, you can reapply adhesive where necessary. A damp sponge may be used to restore the tackiness to the adhesive.

Flocked wallpaper requires special care when hanging. Use a medium-nap paint roller to apply adhesive directly to the wall surface, no more than 1/2 inch beyond the area to be covered by the strip. For areas where the roller will not reach (ceiling line for example), use a small paint brush to apply the adhesive. Hang the wallpaper immediately and smooth with a clean, medium-nap paint roller. Be especially careful to keep the paint roller clean at all times. Always remove excess adhesive from the wallpaper seams with clean water and a sponge.

Foil and Mylar wallpapers require an almost perfect wall surface. Special handling is required to prevent scratching or creasing. Hang this type of wallpaper as you would flocks. Consider using Imperial Wallcover first if your walls are in bad shape.

The "wet look" vinyls require a smooth, unblemished wall surface. The glossy surface of these wallpapers makes any defect on the wall more obvious. After they are hung, they should not be touched for several hours.

Save extra wallpaper; it may come in handy someday for patching damaged areas. To patch, cut a piece from wallpaper scraps; make it larger than the damaged area. Paste or tape it right on top of the damaged area with the pattern matching. With a razor knife, cut through both the patch and the original covering. Peel off the old section and paste in the new patch.

Occasionally a seam or corner of your wallpaper may come unglued. This is a common occurrence in areas of high moisture. The best remedy for such ills is regluing. Peel the wallpaper slightly until you feel some resistance. Then apply some white household glue to the surface of the wall. Press the paper back into place and hold it there with a thumb tack. Wipe off any excess glue. After 24 hours remove the thumb tack; the wallpaper should remain in place for years.

To remove strippable wallpaper, loosen a top corner, then pull the strip back, parallel to the wall. This prevents plaster from pulling away with the paper. Paste residue clinging to the wall is water soluble; just wipe it off.

To add a decorator's touch to your walls, you can cover switch plates, window shades, valances, or picture frames with wallpaper.

Cover the light switch plates in the room with wallpaper that matches or accents the paper on the walls. First remove the plate. Cut out a rectangle of wallpaper that is larger than the plate. Paste the rectangle onto the front of the plate. Fold the edges of the paper over the back of the plate and miter the corners. Cut out a slot for the switch lever. Secure the paper to the plate with rubberbands until the paste dries. Trim off the excess paper. Take special precautions when applying metallic foils to switch plates: Foils must be securely fastened to the face of the plate so there will be no contact between the foil and the wires.

Wooden objects (valances, frames, etc.) can be easily covered with wallpaper. Wallpaper can be pulled taut over the front of the object and then stapled to the back. If the staples will show, keep them straight and cover them with decorative rope or lace to match the wallpaper.

Chapter 11
Windows

Windows are a transparent barrier between the inside of your home and the elements outside. Windows help to provide necessary ventilation for your house. They can cut your heat loss, reduce the need for air conditioning, shut out traffic noise, and provide privacy.

Windows in today's homes are chosen more for the view and the light they will let in than for ventilation. The popularity of sliding glass doors will attest to this fact. The truth of the matter is that modern homes with sophisticated heating and air conditioning systems do not really need windows for ventilation. But with the escalating costs of energy to run modern air conditioning systems, more homeowners are using windows to help provide no-cost cooling for their homes.

There are three basic questions that should be answered when considering the purchase of windows: What kind of view will they provide? Do the windows lend themselves to easy cleaning? Will the windows provide adequate ventilation?

TYPES OF WINDOWS, GLASS, FRAMES, AND HARDWARE

There are three basic types of windows; sliding, fixed, and swinging (casement). There are many variations, which we will discuss later. The type of glass, frame, and hardware used in window construction will have an effect on the cost and durability of the window. The following is a list of the various types of glass used in windows as well as the different materials used for frames.

Types of Glass

Single-strength glass

Suitable for small glass panes. Longest dimension is about 40 inches.

Double-strength glass

Thicker, stronger glass suitable for larger panes. Longest dimension is about 60 inches.

Plate glass

Thick and very strong for the largest panes. Free from distortion. Longest dimension is about 10 feet.

Insulating glass

Two layers of glass separated by a dead-air space and sealed at the edges. Desirable for cold climates to reduce heat loss and heating costs. Low noise transmission.

Safety glass

Acrylic or Plexiglas panels that resist breakage. Panels are more prone to scratching than glass.

Types of Frame

Wood

Preferable in cold climates as there is less problem with condensation. Should be treated to resist decay and moisture absorption. Painting needed on outside unless the frame is covered with factory-applied vinyl shield or other good protective coating.

Aluminum	Painting not needed unless color change is desired. Condensation can be a problem in cold climates unless the frame is specially constructed to reduce heat transfer. Often less tight than wood frames.
Steel	Painting is necessary to prevent rusting unless it is stainless steel. Condensation is often a problem in colder climates.
Plastic	Lightweight and corrosion-free. Painting not needed unless a color change is desired.
Hardware	The best handles, hinges, latches, locks, etc., are steel or brass. Aluminum is satisfactory for some items but is often less durable. Some plastics and pot metal are often disappointing and should be avoided.

Fixed (stationary) windows do not require screens or hardware because they cannot be opened. Cleaning fixed windows must be done from the side that needs cleaning. This can be a problem if the window is on the second story of your home. Ventilation is not possible with a fixed window. On the plus side of fixed windows, there is no air leakage and views are unobstructed.

Sliding windows fall into two categories: double-hung and horizontal sliding. Double-hung windows are probably the most common type of window found in homes (Fig. 11-1). Problems usually occur with double-hung windows when they become old and covered with paint or when the window is installed over a sink or counter, making

Fig. 11-1. Double-hung windows. (Courtesy Andersen Corp.)

opening a bit difficult. Cleaning is rarely a problem. Views from double-hung windows are obstructed by the horizontal frame. Ventilation is limited because the window can only be opened halfway.

Horizontal-sliding windows are common in modern house design. The sliding-glass door is a larger version of the sliding-glass window (Fig. 11-2). The window pushes to the side in metal or plastic tracks. Cleaning can sometimes be a problem if the sash cannot be removed. Ventilation is limited to half the total window space because the window can only be opened halfway.

Swinging windows fall into three categories: casement, awning, and jalousie. Casement windows swing out with the aid of a pushbar or crank (Fig. 11-3). A latch locks the sash tightly when closed. Cleaning is simple, providing there is space for an arm on the hinged side. Ventilation is excellent because the window opens fully. Casement windows actually "scoop" air into a house.

Awning windows are available in two types: top-hinged and bottom-hinged. Top-hinged windows swing outward with the aid of a pushbar or crank. Or they may swing inward when used high on a wall. Cleaning is usually a simple inside job, unless the top hinges prevent access to the outside of the glass. Single units offer a clear, unobstructed view. Stacked units have horizontal divisions which reduce the view. Top-hinged windows open fully and provide good upward air flow if opened outward, or a downward air flow if opened inward.

Bottom-hinged awning windows swing inward. They're opened with a simple lock or latch at the top of the window sash. Bottom-hinged awning windows are the easiest to clean because the entire window is inside the house. But, they are not very good "viewing" windows because they are usually set low in a wall for ventilation. Air flow is directed upward.

Jalousie windows are composed of a series of horizontal glass louvers that open outward by turning a crank. Cleaning is an inside job that requires a lot of time because of the many small sections to clean. However, air flow can be adjusted precisely.

WINDOW INSTALLATION

Replacement windows come in all sizes. Window replacement will usually involve removing existing moldings, inside and out. Once the moldings are off, you can see how the window has been nailed

Fig. 11-2. Sliding-glass doors. (Courtesy Andersen Corp.)

into the opening. Some quick work with a crow bar or nail puller and hammer should get the old window out.

Once the old window has been removed, check the size of the rough opening. If you bought a replacement window that was designed to replace a standard-sized window, you simply slip in the new window and install molding and flashing. If, on the other hand, the rough opening is smaller or larger than the replacement window frame, you will have to enlarge or decrease the size of the rough opening. If the opening is too large, you can usually fill the excess with 2 × 4s or similar spacers. If the opening is too small, you will more than likely have to remove one or more wall studs and rebuild to the required dimensions. Manufacturers of replacement windows always supply detailed instructions on how to install windows. Make sure that these directions are included when you purchase replacement windows. Always follow the manufacturer's recommendations when installing the replacement windows.

There is a fair amount of work involved in building a new window into a wall. First you must remove the interior wall covering to expose the wall studs underneath. If the width of the new window is under 4 feet, you can remove two studs without any problem. However, if the rough opening will be greater than 4 feet, you should use some type of bracing, to help carry the weight of the wall.

After the interior wall covering and studs have been removed, make an outline, with a pencil, of the rough opening onto the back of the exterior siding or sheeting. At the four corners of the outline drive nails through to the outside. Next, from the outside, draw connecting lines between the nail holes so you have an outline of the rough opening on the exterior wall. Cut out the rough opening with a hand-held circular saw.

After the rough opening has been cut, build the rough opening frame from the inside. To do this, first cut two pieces of header material to fit into the rough opening. Nail the two pieces together, using thick enough spacers to make the header thickness equal the width of the wall studs (Fig. 11-4). Nail the header into the opening at the desired height (Fig. 11-5). Cut jack studs to fit under the header; nail them to the regular studs (Fig. 11-6). Measure the height of the rough opening (from the header to the proposed rough sill) and mark this distance on the jack studs. The rough sill is not just nailed to the jack studs; it must also be supported by short 2 × 4s

Fig. 11-3. Casement windows. (Courtesy Andersen Corp.)

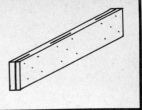

Fig. 11-4. Window header. (Courtesy Andersen Corp.)

(cripples). Cut the cripples and the rough sill to the proper length and nail them in place (Fig. 11-7). Toenail the cripples to the bottom plate. Apply exterior sheathing (plywood, fiberboard, etc.) directly to the rough opening framing members (Fig. 11-8).

Once the frame has been built, checked for squareness, and nailed into place, lay the new window into position. If required, flashing is installed above the window on the exterior of the house. Exterior molding or trim is also installed on the exterior wall if required. The outside of the window is finished with caulking around all the edges.

From the inside, insulation material is stapled and packed all around the window. The interior wall is then covered with either replacement or salvaged (from the original wall) wall covering material. Installation of interior molding around the window finishes the job.

Installation of sliding-glass doors requires slightly more work. Besides working with a larger area, the installation of a sliding-glass door often requires some type of floor refinishing and a porch or steps for the outside.

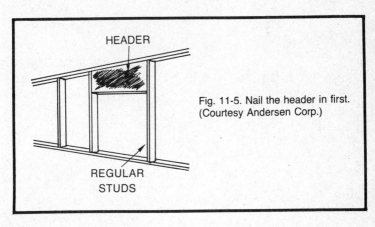

HEADER

REGULAR STUDS

Fig. 11-5. Nail the header in first. (Courtesy Andersen Corp.)

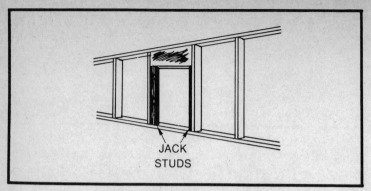

JACK
STUDS

Fig. 11-6. Jack studs help to support the header. (Courtesy Andersen Corp.)

Begin installing a sliding glass door the same way you would install a new window: Remove the interior wall covering and the required number of studs. Frame out the rough opening with 2 × 4s and a header. After you have constructed a rough opening of the size required, set the frame of the sliding-glass door in place. Caulking compound is run across the opening to provide a tight seal between the door sill and the floor. The jamb must be plumb and straight, so check as you nail.

After the entire door frame has been nailed into place, flashing is attached over the top of the door frame. The glass doors are then

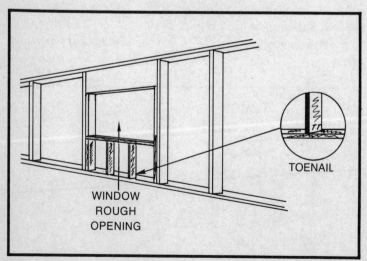

TOENAIL

WINDOW
ROUGH
OPENING

Fig. 11-7. Nail the cripples and the rough sill into place. (Courtesy Andersen Corp.)

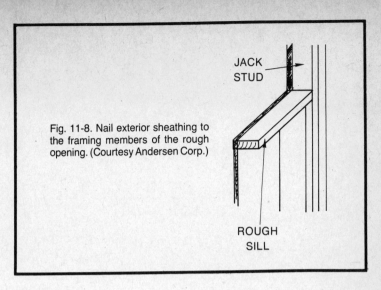

JACK
STUD

Fig. 11-8. Nail exterior sheathing to the framing members of the rough opening. (Courtesy Andersen Corp.)

ROUGH
SILL

put into the frame and checked for operation. Exterior wall coverings and molding are installed. From the inside, insulation is packed and stapled around the door. Interior wall covering is attached as well as molding.

Chapter 12
Room Dividers

Room dividers offer unlimited possibilities for home remodeling. For example, a room that is too large can be divided into smaller, more functional areas by building in one or more solid dividers or translucent partitions. Partitions can also be built to conceal stairways or specific work areas, such as the laundry or workshop. The problem of drafty rooms can often be remedied by simply building a partition in front of the main entrance. Many commercial buildings do this; heat loss and drafts are reduced considerably.

Room dividers are used in many offices and factories. It has been proven that worker efficiency increases when work areas are partitioned off in some way.

Living rooms in many homes are large inefficient areas. Often a section will be used as a dining area, and other sections will be used for viewing television, conversation, and entertaining. If a room divider were built to section off, say, the dining area from the rest of the living room, there would be two separate atmospheres, for two different functions. Of course, not all living rooms lend themselves to division, but there are other possibilities, such as half-walls or translucent partitions. Consider the larger rooms in your home. Could they be divided for more effective and efficient use of space?

If, when you think of room dividers, the only thing that comes to mind is a solid wall, you are in for some surprises. A room divider is anything that separates one area from another; thus, even a long couch could be considered a room divider. Dividers can also be decorative screens, book shelves, or fiberglass panels. Solid walls, 3 to 4 feet high, that run part way across a room make attractive and useful room dividers. The possibilities are endless.

PLANNING ROOM DIVISION

The first step in building a room divider, as with any home remodeling project, is to formulate a workable plan. Make a scale floor plan of the room and position furnishings, in their approximate locations, on the plan. Usually the location of a room divider is easy to determine; in fact, it is often dictated by the furnishings and shape of the room. But what type of divider would be best for your room? Full wall, half-wall, screen, bookcase, planter? Consider all the possibilities and decide which type of divider will best suit your needs.

Natural lighting will be affected if a solid divider is installed. Heating and air circulation will also be affected by any type of partition, so plan accordingly. Another point to consider is the furnishings you already own. Will they be as functional if the room is divided?

THE VARIETY OF DIVIDERS

By far, the most common room divider is a solid wall. The building of conventional walls was discussed in Chapter 1. In this chapter we will concern ourselves with room dividers other than conventional walls.

Half-walls can be constructed horizontally or vertically. Horizontal half-walls are generally 3 to 4 feet high. It is common to have cabinet storage space as the base of horizontal half-walls. The top of this type of room divider can be covered with tile or plastic laminate and used as a counter or work area. Another possible use for the top of a horizontal half-wall is a place to keep house plants. Often, bookcases or shelves are built on top and function as both a room divider and a display area. Stereo units and television sets might also be located on top of a horizontal half-wall.

Vertical half-walls run from floor to ceiling and prevent movement or visual contact between two areas. These walls are usually just an extension of a conventional wall, say at the end of a hallway. Vertical half-walls also work well on both sides of doors to the outside or at the bottom of a stairwell.

Fig. 12-1. A screened partition. (Courtesy Barclay Industries, Inc.)

A partition is usually a thin or translucent divider that helps to section off rooms, but does not offer any sound proofing or strength. Often, a partition consists of a wooden or metal frame that holds a translucent fiberglass panel or decorative grillwork (Fig. 12-1). Barclay Industries, 64 Industrial Road, Lodi, New Jersey, offers a wide selection of decorative and fiberglass panels. Barclay also has easy-to-assemble moldings and quality accessories specially designed for holding the panels (Fig. 12-2).

BUILDING YOUR OWN DIVIDERS

Probably the simplest type of homemade half-wall is a series of boxes, fastened together with wood screws. Build the boxes from 3/4-inch sheets of high-quality (sanded on both sides) interior plywood. Make the dimensions of each box 1 foot high, 1 foot wide,

Fig. 12-2. There is a variety of moldings and panels available. (Courtesy Barclay Industries, Inc.)

and 1 foot deep (outside dimensions). Assemble the boxes with glue and finishing nails, filling the nail holes and exposed edges of each box. After you have assembled enough boxes to make the half-wall you require, nail or screw the first or bottom row of boxes directly to the floor. If you want the bottom of the half-wall to be raised a few inches off the floor, you can make a platform and attach it to the floor before stacking the boxes.

Working with 1-foot square modular boxes leaves lots of room for variation. You can add doors to some of the boxes (sliding or hinged). You can even make one of the boxes into a wine rack by inserting some type of grillwork. Thin vertical partitions (1/4-inch plywood) spaced at 2-inch intervals inside a box would make the ideal place to store record albums.

Instead of building your own boxes, you can use plastic or wooden milk cases. These cases are sturdy and come in assorted colors (green, blue, red, and orange). The cases should be bolted together for rigidity. About the only woodwork necessary is a 4- by 8-foot sheet of 1/4-inch plywood cut to fit onto the back for added strength and appearance.

There are several other kinds of half-walls that can be constructed. Build a half-wall frame from 2 × 4s and cover it with paneling, gypsum board, packing crates, or barn siding. In effect, what you are building is a counter; the inside is for storage and the top can either be a work space or plant area.

Try building a half-wall/counter in the kitchen, in the center of the floor. Build a half-wall with a comfortable working height, approximately 4 feet square (if space permits). The bottom can serve as extra storage space (there's never enough in the kitchen), and the top can serve as a work counter. Cover the top with plastic laminate, tile, or wooden 2- by 2-inch strips (for the butcher-block look).

If you decide that a partition would be better suited for your home, you can, as I mentioned earlier, buy moldings and panels that will fit together. Or you can build your own partition, which is nothing more than a frame built to house a translucent, decorative, or solid panel.

A simple floor-to-ceiling partition can be constructed from 2- by 3-inch and 1- by 2-inch stock (Fig. 12-3). Cut the stock to the proper size. Special care should be given to the half-lap cuts on the ends of the 2- by 3-inch stock; square cuts will give a tight fitting joint.

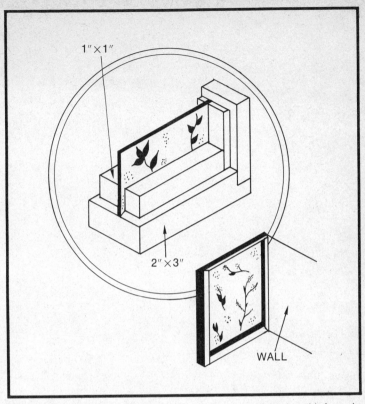

Fig. 12-3. The partition itself is held in place by 1- by 1-inch lumber; this frame is enclosed by 2- by 3-inch lumber. (Courtesy Barclay Industries, Inc.)

Assemble the entire frame, including panel, on the floor and tilt it into position. Unfortunately, most ceilings will not permit this without damage to the ceiling or frame. Therefore, it is best to attach the bottom of the frame to the floor first. Use a plumb line to determine the proper position for the top (ceiling) plate. Nail the top plate to the ceiling. Then attach the 2- by 3-inch uprights to the top and bottom plates. The half-lap joints should be joined with a combination of glue and finishing nails.

Next, attach the 1- by 1-inch stock to the inside of the frame. Using a combination of glue and small finishing nails or wire brads, attach one side of the interior frame (1- by 1-inch stock). It will save time later and make the work easier if you cut both sides of the inside frame at the same time. After half the inside frame has been attached to the 2- by 3-inch outside frame, place the panel into the frame.

Attach the other half of the interior frame, then the upper and lower portions.

Countersink and fill all nail holes with a suitable putty or filler. After the filler has dried, you can either stain the frame to match other woodwork in the room or you can paint it. Remember that all bare woods must be primed before a coat of paint is applied.

Chapter 13
Sound Conditioning

In the beginning there was—well, relative quiet. But since the Industrial Revolution there has been an endless, perturbing, inescapable onslaught of automated clanging, banging, grinding, hissing, and booming—the incessant noises of the factory, the automobile, the supersonic jet, and the labor-saving machine. At first, all this commotion was reluctantly accepted as the price of progress, the byproduct of expanding capability. Now the joke's up: In the midst of this bombardment of sound, a lot of people are making their *own* noise—about the harmful effects of excessive sound levels, about the psychological and physiological consequences of living in a world that offends the ear. We now know that excessive noise can cause fatigue, irritability, inefficiency, and a gradual loss of hearing. More importantly, we know there are ways to attack the problem. Home sound conditioning is one of them: It's not a cure-all, just a technique for insuring a little peace and quiet where it counts, on the home front.

THE NATURE OF SOUND

"If a tree falls in a forest, with no one around, does the falling make a sound?" To this ancient, Zenlike question I give you an unequivocal answer: yes and no. This can be the *only* answer because sound has a dual nature. It has both a physical and a physiological aspect. In physical terms, sound is a wavelike vibration or disturbance in a medium, like air for instance. Physiologically, sound is an auditory sensation produced by such a disturbance. Thus I say yes: The tree's falling produces wave motion in the air. And I say no: Despite the presence of sound waves in the forest, no ears hear, no sound is preceived. To be concerned about sound conditioning is to be concerned about both these aspects of sound.

So let's begin by stating the obvious. The sensation of sound requires three things: (1) a source of sound, something that produces a vibration; (2) a medium to transmit the vibration; and (3) an ear to perceive the transmitted vibrations. Drop a stone into a placid pool of water. Concentric water waves will emanate from the point where the stone plops, moving outward on the face of the pool. Sound behaves much the same way. When a source gives off sound, the medium—air or glass or walls whatever—vibrates with waves of pressure, sound waves that travel in all directions. If these waves impinge against an eardrum, sound is perceived.

Sound can travel through any *elastic* medium (any material that will vibrate—that includes every stud and wall and window of your house). It follows, then, that sound *cannot* move through a vacuum, which is the absence of a medium. If you mount an electric buzzer inside a sealed bell jar and flip the switch, you'll be able to hear the buzzer loud and clear. But if you gradually pump the air out of the jar, the sound of the buzzer will wane until it is inaudible. No medium, no sound. Pump the air back in—that is, give the sound a medium—and you'll hear the buzz again.

We all know that sound travels at a finite rate; that is, the transmission of sound is not an instantaneous process. If we watch a rifle being fired far away, we'll see the flash before we hear the boom. Common knowledge. But we should also know that the speed of sound varies considerably, depending on the medium through which it is moving. Through air, sound travels at 1087 feet per second (when the air is 32° F); through glass, 18,050 feet per second. And through your walls, sound will pass at a very different rate, depending on what your walls are made of.

The most obvious parameter of sound is *loudness* (or intensity, as acoustical experts would say). To accurately gauge this factor, scientists have introduced the decibel (dB), a unit of measurement equivalent to the smallest change in sound intensity that can be detected by the human ear. Figure 13-1 illustrates the full range of

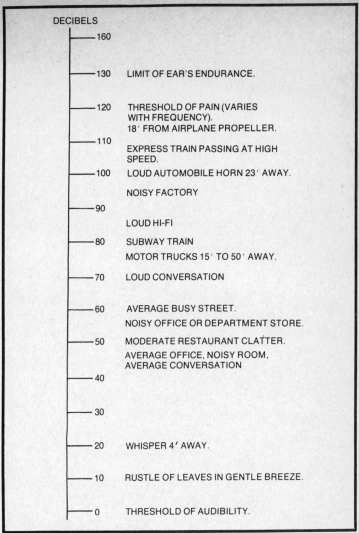

DECIBELS

160	
130	LIMIT OF EAR'S ENDURANCE.
120	THRESHOLD OF PAIN (VARIES WITH FREQUENCY). 18′ FROM AIRPLANE PROPELLER.
110	EXPRESS TRAIN PASSING AT HIGH SPEED.
100	LOUD AUTOMOBILE HORN 23′ AWAY.
	NOISY FACTORY
90	
	LOUD HI-FI
80	SUBWAY TRAIN
	MOTOR TRUCKS 15′ TO 50′ AWAY.
70	LOUD CONVERSATION
60	AVERAGE BUSY STREET. NOISY OFFICE OR DEPARTMENT STORE.
50	MODERATE RESTAURANT CLATTER. AVERAGE OFFICE, NOISY ROOM, AVERAGE CONVERSATION
40	
30	
20	WHISPER 4′ AWAY.
10	RUSTLE OF LEAVES IN GENTLE BREEZE.
0	THRESHOLD OF AUDIBILITY.

Fig. 13-1. Audibility range of the human ear.

our audibility, in decibels. We can hardly perceive sounds at 0 dB; sounds louder than 120 dB hurt our ears and can actually damage our hearing.

WALLS AND STC RATINGS

What happens to airborne sound when it hits your walls? Well, three things. First, some of the sound is reflected off the wall

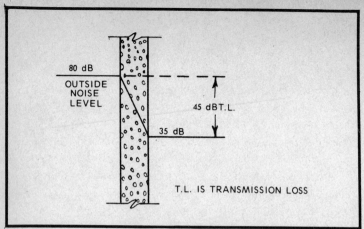

Fig. 13-2. This wall can reduce the level of impinging sound by 45 dB.

surfaces, bouncing back very much as light bounces off a mirror. Second, some of the sound is absorbed into the wall materials. And third, a lot of the sound is transmitted through the wall.

Let's talk about that third point. When I say that sound is *transmitted* through the wall, I don't mean that vibrating air molecules penetrate wallboard and studs. I refer to airborne sound's ability to set a wall to vibrating: Sound waves vibrate air molecules, which in turn start wall molecules dancing, transferring the sound vibrations all the way through the wall to the other side.

Of course, by the time the sound gets through the wallboard, studs, or whatever, its intensity will be reduced: It won't seem nearly as loud. This reduction of intensity is called *transmission loss* (TL). Transmission loss is a pretty useful notion, for it helps us gauge the sound-muffling capability of various mediums. If a wall has a TL factor of 45 dB, an 80 dB sound will be reduced to 35 dB in passing through it (Fig. 13-2). In more pragmatic terms: If an exterior house wall has a 60 dB TL factor, and the street noises outside the wall are a constant 80 dB, the wall can "screen" that clamor to 20 dB (Fig. 13-3).

For simplicity's sake, the above explanation is rather casual. The *whole* truth is that TL factors can vary according to sound frequency. When it comes to muffling a sound of frequency X, a certain wall may have a TL factor of 25 dB. But as a shield against sounds of frequency Y, the same wall may have a TL factor of 50 dB. So if we want a rating of the *overall* sound-stopping capability of our walls, we'll have to find another measure, one that takes into account all kinds of frequencies.

Well, the American Society for Testing Materials has come up with such a measure: *Sound Transmission Class* (STC). An STC rating is an estimate of the overall resistance of a building element (such as a wall) to the passage of airborne sound. It's an evaluation of a material's power to resist vibration—to resist when sound waves are moving through the air and bombarding the material's molecules. STC is similar to TL, but a lot more definitive, a lot more useful.

STC ratings couldn't be more straightforward: the higher the rating, the better the sound-stopping capability. If you were in a room whose walls had an STC rating of 25, you could easily hear people talking in the next room. If the walls had a rating of 35, loud speech in the adjacent room would be audible but not intelligible. Walls with a rating of 45: You'd have to strain to even hear loud speech. STC 50: As quiet as a tomb. Beyond STC 50 you're approaching true soundproofing, the absence of all sound.

The above suggests a norm—or something to shoot for. Exterior walls in houses and apartments should have an STC rating of at least 45. Walls with this minimum rating can muffle the din of civilization, unless they happen to be within 100 feet of an oft-used railroad track.

But how can we boost a wall's STC rating? There are only two ways to do it: (1) Increase the wall's density, or (2) change the wall's

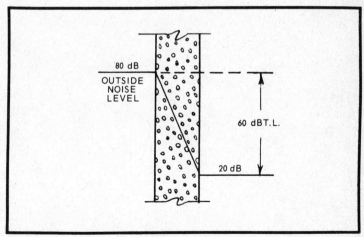

Fig. 13-3. This wall has a TL of 60 dB, which makes it a powerful sound muffler.

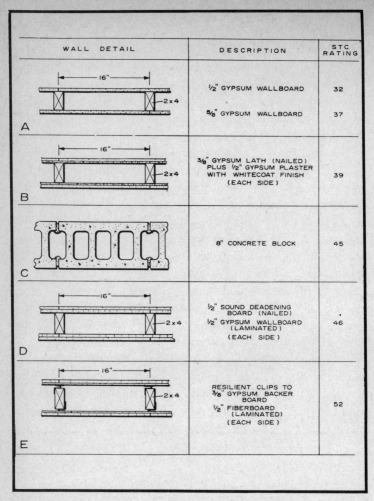

WALL DETAIL	DESCRIPTION	STC RATING
A	1/2" GYPSUM WALLBOARD	32
	5/8" GYPSUM WALLBOARD	37
B	3/8" GYPSUM LATH (NAILED) PLUS 1/2" GYPSUM PLASTER WITH WHITECOAT FINISH (EACH SIDE)	39
C	8" CONCRETE BLOCK	45
D	1/2" SOUND DEADENING BOARD (NAILED) 1/2" GYPSUM WALLBOARD (LAMINATED) (EACH SIDE)	46
E	RESILIENT CLIPS TO 3/8" GYPSUM BACKER BOARD 1/2" FIBERBOARD (LAMINATED) (EACH SIDE)	52

Fig. 13-4. STC ratings for various wall constructions.

composition. Increasing wall density means adding weight; the heavier the wall, the greater its resistance to airborne sound. This doesn't mean, however, that an 8-inch thick concrete wall will necessarily have a higher STC rating than a conventional wall covered with lightweight sound-deadening materials. It just means that 4 inches of wall is better than 2 inches. And that presages point 2. The composition of a wall—its structural configuration, the nature of its materials—has a tremendous effect on the STC rating, a fact that rings with significance for the homeowner. High-density (heavy)

190

walls are expensive and sometimes architecturally impractical (they put a big strain on the floors). But changing the way a wall is put together is a relatively easy, economically sensible method of hiking up the STC number.

A conventional wall composed of 2- by 4-inch studs and 1/2-inch gypsum wallboard has an STC rating of 32 (Fig. 13-4A). A conventional wall covered with 5/8-inch gypsum wallboard isn't much better—an STC rating of 37. But change that skeletal composition just a bit and you can increase the rating without adding substantially to construction costs. Cover those wall studs with 3/8-inch gypsum lath plus 1/2 inch of gypsum plaster (with whitecoat finish): That'll bring the STC rating up to 39 (Fig. 13-4B).

Some folks find an STC rating of 39 quite tolerable. Nevertheless, it's a far cry from the norm of 45. Eight-inch-thick concrete block walls can give you an STC rating of 45, but they're also expensive. Not pleasant to look at either. Fortunately, it is possible to achieve the norn (and exceed it) without a lot of expense. Figure 13-4D illustrates one way to do it. If you nail 1/2-inch sound-deadening board to your wall studs (both sides) and then glue on some 1/2-inch gypsum wallboard, you'll get an STC rating of 46. And if you use 5/8-inch gypsum wallboard instead of the 1/2-inch stuff, you can boost the STC rating a bit more.

Some homeowners—notably stereo enthusiasts and peace-and-quiet lovers—demand much higher STC ratings, way above 46. They crave chamberlike tranquility. They want to be surrounded by walls that could stop the sound of a 747 jetliner in the front yard. Well, such walls probably don't exist, but the construction shown in Fig. 13-4E would be a good substitute. And building it would not be a very costly proposition. Just attach 3/8-inch gypsum backer board to your wall studs (both sides) with special resilient clips, then glue 1/2-inch fiberboard to the backer board. The resilient clips make all the difference in the world. They keep the wall coverings away from the studs, short-circuiting the transmission of sound through the whole structure. The result: a healthy STC rating of 52.

By now you have probably inferred a very important principle of sound conditioning: Since sound needs a medium for transmission, a break or gap in the medium will short circuit the sound waves. Resilient clips are just *one* kind of gap. Another kind is illustrated in Fig. 13-5A. This type of construction is called a *staggered-stud* wall and is, essentially, a way to isolate one side of a wall from the other.

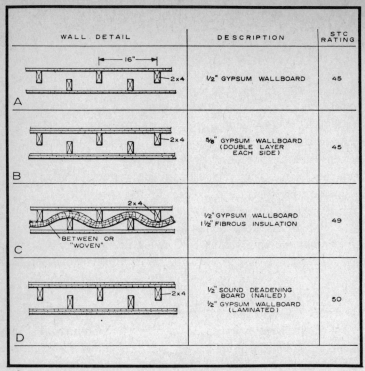

WALL DETAIL	DESCRIPTION	STC RATING
A ←16"→ 2x4	1/2" GYPSUM WALLBOARD	45
B 2x4	5/8" GYPSUM WALLBOARD (DOUBLE LAYER EACH SIDE)	45
C 2x4 BETWEEN OR "WOVEN"	1/2" GYPSUM WALLBOARD 1 1/2" FIBROUS INSULATION	49
D 2x4	1/2" SOUND DEADENING BOARD (NAILED) 1/2" GYPSUM WALLBOARD (LAMINATED)	50

Fig. 13-5. STC ratings for various staggered stud walls.

In a conventional wall, sound can be transmitted through the wall covering to the studs to the otherside of the wall. A direct path. But in a staggered-stud wall, the path is disrupted. And building such a structure is nearly as easy as putting up a conventional wall. You have to use 2- by 6-inch sole plates and regular 2- by 4-inch studs (Fig. 13-6). Cover this framing on both sides with 1/2-inch gypsum wallboard and you have a wall with an STC rating of 45.

There are ways to beef up a staggered-stud wall's rating, but slapping on more gypsum wallboard is not one of them. As Fig. 13-5B shows, even double thicknesses of 5/8-inch wallboard does not significantly affect the wall's STC number.

Experts have discovered, however, that the rating *can* be increased by using thermal insulation (Fig. 13-5C), which *absorbs* sound quite well. When sound waves enter it, some of them reflect back and forth inside the insulation's tiny cavities, dissipating at each bounce. In configurations such as the staggered-stud wall, a layer of insulation within the wall cavity can make a lot of difference. Just

1 1/2 inches of good fibrous insulation sandwiched between 1/2-inch thicknesses of gypsum wallboard can boost the STC to 49. You can weave the insulation through the wall cavity (Fig. 13-5C) or fasten it to the wallboard (Fig. 13-6).

There are several other variations on the staggered-stud wall theme—all of them practical. If you nail 1/2-inch sound-deadening board to the studs and cover that with 1/2-inch gypsum wallboard, you'll have an STC rating of 50. Add thermal insulation to this construction (in the cavity) and the rating will jump to 53 or beyond.

Keep in mind that the whole point of the staggered-stud construction is to break up sound's medium, to create a gap in the wall cavity. Let one piece of electrical conduit or an outlet box span the gap and you undermine the whole works.

SOUND ABSORPTION

Usually, being in an empty room (no drapes, no furniture, no rugs) is like being in an echo chamber. When you speak, your voice

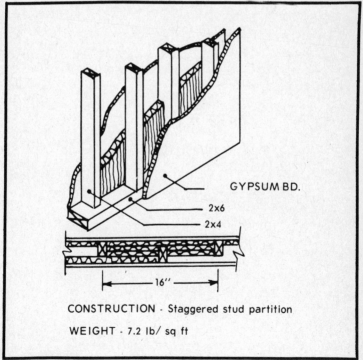

GYPSUM BD.

2x6

2x4

16"

CONSTRUCTION - Staggered stud partition

WEIGHT - 7.2 lb/ sq ft

Fig. 13-6. Cutaway of a staggered-stud wall.

bounces off the walls, off the floor, off the ceiling, reflecting from surface to surface. The annoying echo persists because there is little or nothing in the room to absorb the sound. Even when you furnish such a room from end to end, you may still be able to detect some reverberation—which usually means that the room is "noisy," a persistent irritation.

Thus a truly quiet house must have more than a lot of walls with high STC ratings—it must have the capability of absorbing sound generated from within. Drapes and rugs help, but if you really cherish quietude, you'll have to use special sound-absorbing materials.

Acoustic tiles are the most common sound-absorbers around. You've seen them on the walls and ceilings of auditoriums, workshops, playrooms, dens, and living rooms. They're usually made from wood fiber, treated with fire-resisting chemicals. The surfaces of the tiles are peppered with tiny holes—miniature sound traps that swallow up sound and minimize its reflection back into rooms. Technically, these holes catch sound waves and dissipate their energy as friction-generated heat.

For the sake of simplicity I have been simplistic, again. The fact is, acoustic tiles (and all other sound-absorbing materials) absorb certain frequencies better than others. Such a qualifier probably won't mean much to the average homeowner, but if you're a hi-fi/stereo/quad/supersound freak, that tidbit of information will be of supreme importance. A concrete wall covered with standard 1/2-inch-thick cellulose acoustic tiles will do a great job of absorbing high-frequency sound, but a lousy job of soaking up low-frequency sound. Treble frequencies will be muffled; bass frequencies will not; the imbalance will drive any audioiphile to distraction.

For the audio enthusiast, acoustic tiles aren't bad; they're just tricky. Used correctly, tiles can help you get the kind of sound you're after without a lot of expense. But the complexities of designing an efficient, quality listening room are downright intimidating, at least for the amateur. So before you begin cementing acoustic tiles to your walls, make sure you're aware of the acoustic dyamics involved.

Most homeowners, though, need not concern themselves about such dynamics. Getting rid of annoying sounds, of whatever frequency, is the main objective—and most acoustic tiles help to do just that.

You can buy acoustic tiles in a lot of different sizes, from 12 by 12 inches to 24 by 48 inches, from 1/2 to 3/4 inch thick. They're lightweight, prefinished, and chromatically bland. And, unfortunately, you can't paint them: painting clogs up the tiny holes that absorb the sound. Dirt can stop up the holes too, so you'll have to vacuum them occasionally.

In general, you can apply acoustic tiles to a wall faster than you can paint it. (Often a good paint job requires more than one coat, and a lot of waiting in between.) Usually it's just a matter of spreading a special mastic adhesive on the wall and interlocking the tiles into place. Make sure, though, that the wall is smooth and flat—and, as always, follow the manufacturer's instructions.

DOORS AND WINDOWS

Sound cannot only move around corners—it can seep through cracks and crevices, through the smallest space around doors and windows. And a little seepage can make a big difference. Opening a window just 1/4 of an inch can bring in almost as much noise as

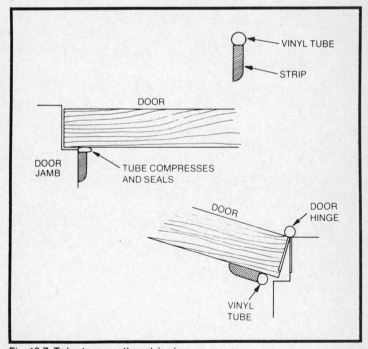

Fig. 13-7. Tube-type weather stripping.

195

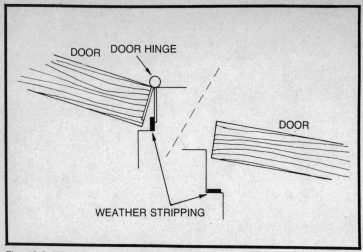

Fig. 13-8. When you close the door, the strips will be squeezed between the door and the stop, sealing off the sound channels.

opening it all the way. So a few crannies around a door or window can undo a lot of sound-conditioning.

The easiest way to reduce sound seepage around doors (both interior and exterior) is to weatherstrip them. Weather-stripping is a technique made to order for people with tight budgets and precious little spare time. It doesn't matter much what kind of weather-stripping material you use; the important thing is to get a good seal. Airtight.

Tube-type weather stripping is being used a lot these days—it's easy to install and wears well. It consists of vinyl tubing attached to a wooden or aluminum mounting strip (Fig 13-7). The idea is to fasten this kind of stripping to either the door or its jamb so that the tube will be compressed when the door is shut, forming a hermetic seal. Actual installation can take as little as 20 minutes. First close the door tight. Place the stripping against the jamb or the door (Fig. 13-7) and slide it until the tubing compresses against the opposing surface. Press hard enough to flatten the tubing a bit. Fasten the stripping in place with nails or screws.

Strips of felt, foam rubber, and plastic make fine weather stripping too—and you can buy them at any hardware store or make your own. Fasten these along the door stop (Fig. 13-8). You can tack the felt strips in place; the store-bought foam rubber and plastic strips have adhesive backing so you can press them into position.

196

Don't forget the thresholds—sound can slip *under* the door too. Actually, stopping this kind of seepage is no big deal: These days you can buy metal/vinyl thresholds that install easily and provide airtight seals. The most popular type consists of an aluminum strip with a vinyl insert (Fig. 13-9A). The whole affair is designed to replace wooden thresholds, which usually do a poor job of butting snug against the bottom edges of doors. To insure a good seal, you may have to shim up these modern thresholds.

The alternative to installing a new threshold is attaching some kind of weather seal to the bottom edge of the door (Fig. 13-9B). Most store-bought weather seals, like the new thresholds, are aluminum and vinyl—which means they'll probably last forever, or close to it. To get these seals to fit properly, you may have to plane a bit off either the bottom edge of the door or the old threshold.

There are lots of ways to weather-strip a window—some of them expensive, some of them remarkably elaborate. But generally, for sound-conditioning purposes, the inexpensive, simple methods are quite adequate.

Take a look at Fig. 13-10. It's a cross section of one side of a standard double-hung window. As you can see, there's an air space

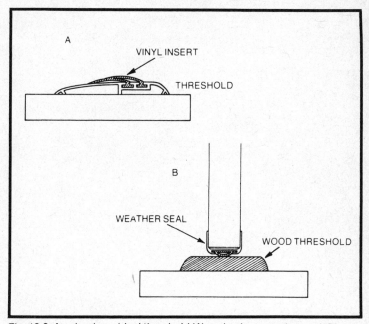

Fig. 13-9. An aluminum/vinyl threshold (A) and a door weather seal (B).

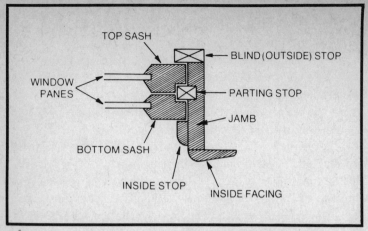

Fig. 13-10. To block the sound channels in a double-hung window, you have to seal off the air space between the jamb and the sashes.

between the jamb and the sashes—a perfect channel for noise infiltration. So the object is to block these channels—and you can do this easily with felt strips. First push the bottom sash against the parting stops. Then tack or glue felt strips along the inside stops, making sure that the strips' edges press hard against the sash. Next, press the top sash against the blind (outside) stops and place felt strips along the parting stops, butting the felt against the top sash. Glue or nail the strips down.

Double-hung windows also have air spaces between their meeting rails (where the bottom and top sashes come together). You can seal off these crevices by filling them with household caulking, felt strips, or special "soft" caulking compound. The drawback, of course, is that you have to remove these materials to raise the windows. So these techniques are, for the most part, wintertime measures.

Glossary

Acoustical tiles. Soft, lightweight fibrous tiles which absorb sound waves.

Acoustics. A science that deals with the production, control, transmission, reception, and effects of sound.

Base or baseboard. A board placed around a room against the wall next to the floor to finish properly between floor and plaster or dry wall.

Base molding. Molding used to trim the upper edge of interior baseboard.

Base shoe. Molding used next to the floor on interior baseboard. Sometimes called a carpet strip.

Batten. Narrow strips of wood used to cover joints or as decorative vertical members over plywood or wide boards.

Beam. A structural member transversely supporting a load.

Bearing partition. A partition that supports any vertical load in addition to its own weight.

Bearing wall. A wall that supports any vertical load in addition to its own weight.

Bed molding. A molding in an angle, as between the over-hanging cornice, or eaves, of a building and the sidewalls.

Blind-nailing. Nailing in such a way that the nailheads are not visible on the face of the work. Usually at the tongue of matched boards.

Blind stop. A rectangular molding, usually 3/4 by 1 3/8 inches or more in width, used in the assembly of a window frame. Serves as a stop for storm and screen or combination windows and to resist air infiltration.

Boiled linseed oil. Linseed oil in which enough lead, manganese, or cobalt salts have been incorporated to make the oil harden more rapidly when spread in thin coatings.

Bolts, anchor. Bolts to secure a wooden sill plate to concrete or masonry floor or wall or pier.

Brace. An inclined piece of framing lumber applied to wall or floor to stiffen the structure. Often used on walls as temporary bracing until framing has been completed.

Buck. Often used in reference to rough frame opening members. Door bucks used in reference to metal door frame.

Butt joint. The junction where the ends of two timbers or other members meet in a square-cut joint.

Casement frames and sash. Frames of wood or metal enclosing part or all of the sash, which may be opened by means of hinges affixed to the vertical edges.

Casing. Molding of various widths and thicknesses used to trim door and window openings at the jambs.

Collar beam. Nominal 1- or 2-inch-thick members connecting opposite roof rafters. They serve to stiffen the roof structure.

Combination doors or windows. Combination doors or windows used over regular openings. They provide winter insulation and summer protection. They often have self-storing or removable glass and screen inserts. This eliminates the need for handling a different unit each season.

Concrete, plain. Concrete without reinforcement, or reinforced only for shrinkage or temperature changes.

Condensation. Beads or drops of water, and frequently frost in extremely cold weather, that accumulate on the inside of the exterior covering of a building when warm, moisture-laden air from the interior reaches a point where the temperature no longer permits the air to sustain the moisture it holds. Use of louvers or attic ventilators will reduce moisture condensation in attics. A vapor barrier under the gypsum lath or dry wall on exposed walls will reduce condensation in walls.

Construction, dry-wall. A type of construction in which the interior wall finish is applied in a dry condition, generally in the form of sheet materials or wood paneling, as contrasted to plaster.

Construction, frame. A type of construction in which the structural parts are of wood or depend upon a wood frame for support. In building codes, if masonry veneer is applied to the exterior walls, the classification of this type of construction is usually unchanged.

Coped joint. Fitting woodwork to an irregular surface. In moldings, cutting the end of one piece to fit the molded face of the other at an interior angle to replace a miter joint.

Corner bead. A strip of formed sheet metal, sometimes combined with a strip of metal lath, placed on corners before plastering to reinforce them. Also, a strip of wood finish three-quarters round or angular placed over a plastered corner for protection.

Corner braces. Diagonal braces at the corners of frame structure to stiffen and strengthen the wall.

Cornice. Overhang of a pitched roof at the eave line, usually consisting of a facia board, a soffit for a closed cornice, and appropriate moldings.

Cove molding. A molding with a concave face used as trim or to finish interior corners.

Dado. A rectangular groove across the width of a board or plank. In interior decoration, a special type of wall treatment.

Decibel. A unit of measurement of sound.

Deck paint. An enamel with a high degree of resistance to mechanical wear, designed for use on such surfaces as porch floors.

Density. The mass of substance in a unit volume. When expressed in the metric system (in g per cc), it is numerically equal to the specific gravity of the same substance.

Doorjamb, interior. The surrounding case into and out of which a door closes and opens. It consists of two upright pieces, called side jambs, and a horizontal head jamb.

Dressed and matched (tongued and grooved). Boards or planks machined in such a manner that there is a groove on one edge and a corresponding tongue on the other.

Drier, paint. Usually oil-soluble soaps of such metals as lead, maganese, or cobalt, which, in small proportions, hasten the oxidation and hardening (drying) of the drying oils in paints.

Face nailing. To nail perpendicular to the initial surface or to the junction of the pieces joined.

Facia or fascia. A flat board, band, or face, used sometimes by itself but usually in combination with moldings, often located at the outer face of the cornice.

Flat paint. An interior paint that contains a high proportion of pigment, and dries to a flat or lusterless finish.

Fly rafter. End rafters of the gable overhang supported by roof sheathing and lookouts.

Footing. A masonry section, usually concrete, in a rectangular form wider than the bottom of the foundation wall or pier it supports.

Foundation. The supporting portion of a structure below the first-floor construction, or below grade, including the footings.

Framing, balloon. A system of framing a building in which all vertical structural elements of the bearing walls and partitions consist of single pieces extending from the top of the foundation sill plate to the roofplate and to which all floor joists are fastened.

Framing, platform. A system of framing a building in which floor joists of each story rest on the top plates of the story below or on the foundation sill for the first story, and the bearing walls and partitions rest on the subfloor of each story.

Frieze. In house construction, a horizontal member connecting the top of the siding with the soffit of the cornice or roof sheathing.

Frostline. The depth of frost penetration in soil. This depth varies in different parts of the country. Footings should be placed below this depth to prevent movement.

Furring. Strips of wood or metal applied to a wall or other surface to even it and usually to serve as a fastening base for finish material.

Gable. The triangular vertical end of a building formed by the eaves and ridge of a sloped roof.

Girder. A large or principal beam of wood or steel used to support concentrated loads at isolated points along its length.

Gloss (paint or enamel). A paint or enamel that contains a relatively low proportion of pigment and dries to a sheen or luster.

Grain. The direction, size, arrangement, appearance, or quality of the fibers in wood.

Grain, edge (vertical). Edge-grain lumber has been sawed parallel to the pith of the log and approximately at right angles to the growth rings; i.e., the rings form an angle of 45° or more with the surface of the piece.

Gutter or eave trough. A shallow channel or conduit of metal or wood set below and along the eaves of a house to catch and carry off rainwater from the roof.

Header. (a) A beam placed perpendicular to joists and to which joists are nailed in framing for chimney, stairway, or other opening. (b) A wood lintel.

Heartwood. The wood extending from the pitch to the sapwood, the cells of which no longer participate in the life processes of the tree.

Insulation board, rigid. A structural building board made of wood or cane fiber in 1/2- and 25/32-inch thicknesses. It can be obtained in various size sheets, in various densities, and with several treatments.

Insulation, thermal. Any material high in resistance to heat transmission that, when placed in the walls, ceilings, or floors of a structure, will reduce the rate of heat flow.

Jack rafter. A rafter that spans the distance from the wallplate to a hip, or from a valley to a ridge.

Jamb. The side and head lining of a doorway, window, or other opening.

Joint. The space between the adjacent surfaces of two members or components joined and held together by nails, glue, cement, mortar, or other means.

Joint cement. Usually a powder that is mixed with water, used for joint treatment in gypsum-wallboard finish. Often called "spackle."

Joist. One of a series of parallel beams, usually 2 inches thick, used to support floor and ceiling loads, and supported in turn by larger beams, girders, or bearing walls.

Knot. In lumber, the portion of a branch or limb of a tree that appears on the edge or face of the piece.

Lath. A building material of wood, metal, gypsum, or insulating board that is fastened to the frame of a building to act as a plaster base.

Ledger strip. A strip of lumber nailed along the bottom of the side of a girder on which joists rest.

Light. Space in a window sash for a single pane of glass. Also a pane of glass.

Lintel. A horizontal structural member that supports the load over an opening such as a door or window.

Lumber. Lumber is the product of the sawmill and planing mill not further manufactured other than by sawing, resawing, and passing lengthwise through a standard planing machine, cross cutting to length, and matching.

Lumber, board. Yard lumber less than 2 inches thick and 2 or more inches wide.

Lumber, dimension. Yard lumber from 2 inches to, but not including, 5 inches thick, and 2 or more inches wide. Includes joists, rafters, studs, plank, and small timbers. The actual size dimension of such lumber after shrinking from green dimension and after machining to size or pattern is called the dress size.

Lumber, matched. Lumber that is dressed and shaped on one edge in a grooved pattern and on the other in a tongued pattern.

Lumber, shiplap. Lumber that is edge-dressed to make a close rabbeted or lapped joint.

Lumber, yard. Lumber of those grades, sizes, and patterns which are generally intended for ordinary construction, such as framework and rough coverage of houses.

Masonry. Stone, brick, concrete, hollow-tile, concrete-block, gypsum-block, or other similar building units or materials or a combination of the same, bonded together with mortar to form a wall, pier, buttress, or similar mass.

Miter joint. The joint of two pieces at an angle that bisects the joining angle. For example, the miter joint at the side and head casing at a door opening is made at a 45° angle.

Moisture content of wood. Weight of the water contained in the wood, usually expressed as a percentage of the weight of the ovendry wood.

Molding. A wood strip having a curved or projecting surface used for decorative purposes.

Mortise. A slot cut into a board, plank, or timber, usually edgewise, to receive tenon of another board, plank, or timber to form a joint.

Natural finish. A transparent finish which does not seriously alter the original color or grain of the natural wood. Natural finishes are usually provided by sealers, oils, varnishes, water-repellent preservatives, and other similar materials.

Noise. Unwanted sound, usually at pitch or intensity disturbing to the human ear.

Nonloadbearing wall. A wall supporting no load other than its own weight.

Notch. A crosswise rabbet at the end of a board.

O.C., on center. The measurement of spacing for studs, rafters, joists, and the like in a building from center of one member to the center of the next.

Paint. A combination of pigments with suitable thinners or oils to provide decorative and protective coatings.

Panel. In house construction, a thin flat piece of wood, plywood, or similar material, framed by stiles and rails as in a door or fitted into groves of thicker material with molded edges for decorative wall treatment.

Paper, sheathing or building. A building material, generally paper or felt used in wall and roof construction as a protection against the passage of air and sometimes moisture.

Parting stop or strip. A small wood piece used in the side and head jambs of double-hung windows to separate upper and lower sash.

Partition. A wall that subdivides spaces within any story of a building.

Penny. As applied to nails, it originally indicated the price per hundred. The term now serves as a measure of nail length and is abbreviated by the letter **d**.

Pier. A column of masonry, usually rectangular in horizontal cross section, used to support other structural members.

Pigment. A powdered solid in suitable degree of subdivision for use in paint or enamel.

Plate. Sill plate: a horizontal member anchored to a masonry wall. Sole plate: Bottom horizontal member of a frame wall. Top plate: Top horizontal member of a frame wall supporting ceiling joists, rafters, or other members.

Plumb. Exactly perpendicular; vertical.

Plywood. A piece of wood made of three or more layers of veneer joined with glue and usually laid with the grain of adjoining plies at right angles. Almost always an odd number of plies are used to provide balanced construction.

Primer. The first coat of paint in a paint job that consists of two or more coats; also the paint used for such a first coat.

Putty. A type of cement usually made of whiting and boiled linseed oil, beaten or kneaded to the consistency of dough, and used in sealing glass in sash, filling small holes and crevices in wood, and for similar purposes.

Rafter. One of a series of structural members of a roof designed to support roof loads. The rafters of a flat roof are sometimes called roof joists.

Rafter, hip. A rafter that forms the intersection of an external roof angle.

Rafter, valley. A rafter that forms the intersection of an internal roof angle. The valley rafter is normally made of doubled 2-inch-thick members.

Rail. Cross members of panel doors or of a sash. Also the upper and lower members of a balustrade or staircase extending from one vertical support, such as a post, to another.

Sash. A single light frame containing one or more lights of glass.

Sealer. A finishing material, either clear or pigmented, that is usually applied directly over uncoated wood for the purpose of sealing the surface.

Semigloss paint or enamel. A paint or enamel made with a slight insufficiency of nonvolatile vehicle so that its coating, when dry, has some luster but is not very glossy.

Shake. A thick handsplit shingle, resawed to form two shakes; usually edge grained.

Sheathing. The structural covering, usually wood boards or plywood, used over studs or rafters of a structure. Structural building board is normally used only as wall sheathing.

Shingles. Roof covering of asphalt, asbestos, wood, tile, slate, or other material cut to stock lengths, widths, and thicknesses.

Shingles, siding. Various kinds of shingles, such as wood shingles or shakes and nonwood shingles, that are used over sheathing for exterior sidewall covering of a structure.

Siding. The finish covering of the outside wall of a frame building, whether made of horizontal weatherboards, vertical boards with battens, shingles, or other material.

Siding, bevel (lap siding). Wedge-shaped boards used as horizontal siding in a lapped pattern. This siding varies in butt thickness from 1/2 to 3/4 inch and in widths up to 12 inches. Normally used over some type of sheathing.

Siding, drop. Usually 3/4 inch thick and 6 and 8 inches in width with tongued-and-grooved or shiplap edges. Often used as siding without sheathing in secondary buildings.

Siding, panel. Large sheets of plywood or hardboard which serve as both sheathing and siding.

Sill. The lowest member of the frame of a structure, resting on the foundation and supporting the floor joists or the uprights of the wall. The member forming the lower side of an opening, as a door sill, window sill, etc.

Soffit. Usually the underside covering of an overhanging cornice.

Sound. A vibration energy that sets molecules in motion which stimulates hearing.

Sound absorption. The ability of a material, such as acoustic tiles, to absorb sound waves.

Sound conditioning. The control and reduction of sound by the use of appropriate materials.

Sound transmission class (STC). A number rating that classifies the values of various materials for reducing sound transmission.

Span. The distance between structural supports such as walls, columns, piers, beams, girders, and trusses.

Stain, shingle. A form of oil paint, very thin in consistency, intended for coloring wood with rough surfaces, like shingles, without forming a coating of significant thickness or gloss.

Storm sash or storm window. An extra window usually placed on the outside of an existing window as additonal protection against cold weather.

String, stringer. A timber or other support for cross members in floors or ceilings. In stairs, the support on which the stair treads rest; also stringboard.

Stud. One of a series of slender wood or metal vertical structural members placed as supporting elements in walls and partitions. (Plural: Studs or studding.)

Subfloor. Boards or plywood laid on joists over which a finish floor is to be laid.

Tail beam. A relatively short beam or joist supported in a wall on one end and by a header at the other.

Termite shield. A shield, usually of noncorrodible metal, placed in or on a foundation wall or other mass of masonry or around pipes to prevent passage of termites.

Threshold. A strip of wood or metal with beveled edges used over the finished floor and the sill of exterior doors.

Toenailing. To drive a nail at a slant with the initial surface in order to permit it to penetrate into a second member.

Transmission loss (TL). Measured in decibels, the sound-insulating efficiency and nontransmitting quality of various constructions.

Trim. The finish materials in a building, such as moldings, applied around openings (window trims, door trim) or at the floor and ceiling of rooms (baseboard, cornice, picture molding).

Trimmer. A beam or joist to which a header is nailed in framing for a chimney, stairway, or other opening.

Truss. A frame or jointed structure designed to act as a beam of long span, while each member is usually subjected to longitudinal stress only, either tension or compression.

Turpentine. A volatile oil used as a thinner in paints and as a solvent in varnishes. Chemically, it is a mixture of terpenes.

Undercoat. A coating applied before the finishing or top coats of a paint job. It may be the first of two or the second of three coats. It is sometimes synonymous with "priming coat."

Vapor barrier. Material used to retard the movement of water vapor into walls and prevent condensation in them. Usually considered as having a perm value of less than 1.0. Applied separately over the warm side of exposed walls or as a part of batt or blanket insulation.

Varnish. A thickened preparation of drying oil or drying oil and resin suitable for spreading on surfaces to form continuous, transparent coatings, or for mixing with pigments to make enamels.

Weatherstrip. Narrow or jamb-width sections of thin metal or other material to prevent infiltration of air and moisture around windows and doors.

Appendix I
Lumber Grades

Lumber grading rules are formulated and published by associations of lumber. manufacturers or by official grading and inspection bureaus.

SOFTWOOD LUMBER

Finish or Select grades.—Finish or select grades of lumber generally are named by the letters A, B, C, and D. The A and B grades are nearly always combined as B and Better, so that only three grades are in practical use.

Thus, in lumber for interior and exterior finishing or other similar uses, only B and Better (first grade), C (second grade), and D (third grade) in softwoods need to be considered. However, considerable knotty pine and cedar in third grade are selected for use as paneling.

Common boards.—Grade names for common boards are not uniform for all softwood species. For example, in redwood boards Select is the first grade, Construction the second, Merchantable the third, and Economy the fourth. With such woods as Douglas fir, west coast hemlock, Sitka spruce, and western red cedar, the grade designations are Select Merchantable, Construction, Standard, Utility, and Economy. A different set of board grades described by the Western Wood Products Association bears the names 1 Common, 2

Common, 3 Common, 4 Common, and 5 Common. The same set of grade names and descriptions is used in the Northeast and Lake States for species such as eastern spruce, balsam fir, red and jack pine, eastern hemlock, and northern white cedar. For the southern pines, the board designations are No. 1, No. 2, No. 3, and No. 4.

Dimension lumber.—Light Framing (2 to 4 inches thick, 2 to 4 inches wide) and Joists and Planks (2 to 4 inches thick, 6 inches and wider) are graded for strength to a common set of grade names and descriptions under all six softwood grading rules published in the United States, and under the National Lumber Grades Authority in Canada. The light framing grades are Construction, Standard, and Utility, and the Joist and Plank grades are Select Structural, No. 1, No. 2, and No. 3. There is also a Structural Light Framing category for roof truss and similar applications that has the same grade names as for Joists and Planks. Load-carrying design values vary by species and use category; therefore, it is important to note that common grade names do not imply equal strength or stiffness.

Trade practices.—It has been the practice for the lumber retailer to quote prices and make deliveries on the basis of local grade classification or on his own judgment of what the user needs or will accept. However, there is a growing practice to put indelible marks on all building lumber at the sawmill, stating the grade, species, size, degree of seasoning, and identity of the supplier. The Federal Housing Administration (FHA) and most code authorities require that framing lumber used in the construction of FHA-insured units be so grade-marked.

The softwoods are graded to meet fairly definite building requirements. Select grades of softwoods are based on suitability for natural and paint finishes: A Select and B Select or B and Better are primarily for natural finishes, and C Select and D Select are for paint finishes. The Utility Board and Dimension grades are based primarily on their suitability for general construction and general utility purposes as influenced by the size, tightness, and soundness of knots.

HARDWOOD LUMBER

The wood of the hardwood trees is graded on the basis of factory grades more than for building requirements. Factory grades take into account the yield and size of cuttings with one clear face that can be sawed from the lumber. The two highest factory grades are known as Firsts and Seconds, and are usually sold combined.

Hardwoods for construction are grouped into three general classes: Finish, Construction and Utility Boards, and Dimension. A Finish has one face practically clear, while B Finish allows small surface checks, mineral streaks, and other minor variations.

Construction Boards and Utility Boards have No. 1, No. 2, and No. 3 grades and are based on the amount of wane, checks, knots, and other defects present in each board.

Dimension grades (2 inches thick) are classed as No. 1 and No. 2 depending on the number of defects.

STRENGTH FACTOR

The ordinary grades of building or so-called yard lumber are based on the size, number, and location of the knots, slope of grain, and the like more than on the strength of the clear wood. Common softwood boards used in conventionally constructed houses and other light-frame structures are not related directly to the strength of the unit itself. Rather, sheathing, subflooring, and roof boards supplement the framing system and may also add to the rigidity of the structure.

The main purpose of boards used in the construction of a building is as a covering material. They also facilitate nailing for siding, flooring, and roofing materials. For these purposes they must have some nail-holding properties as well as moderate strength in bending to carry loads between the frame members. Ordinarily, third- and fourth-grade boards are adequate for this purpose.

Finish and Select grade softwood boards are selected for their appearance rather than strength. They are used mainly for trim and finish purposes, and consequently the grade is chosen based on the type of finish used—natural, stained, or painted.

Softwood Dimension lumber is selected because of its strength and its stiffness. Therefore, the size, number, and location of knots are important and related directly to the intended use. In house floors and walls, for example, where construction is designed to minimize vibration and deflection so far as possible, stiffness rather than breaking strength is most important. Generally, grade affects strength more than stiffness; the lower the grade, the lower the strength.

FINISHING AND APPEARANCE FACTOR

The finishing and appearance of wood is normally associated with the various Board grades rather than Dimension grades. With varnish and natural finishes, A and B Select in softwoods (commonly sold as B and Better) and A Finish in hardwoods assure the best appearance. Some pieces in the B and Better grade are practically clear, although the average board contains one or two small surface features that preclude calling it Clear.

Where the very smoothest appearance is not required, second Finish grade in softwoods and hardwoods gives good satisfaction. The number of knots, pitch pockets, and other nonclear features per board in C Select averages about twice that of B and Better; the proportion of these features that are small knots is greater in C Select than in B and Better. Because of its decorative effects, knotty lumber selected from the first and second Common board grades is frequently in demand for paneling.

For painting where wood is not exposed to the weather, the surface features permitted in the second Finish grade are such that they can be well covered by paint if the priming is properly done. The third Finish grade, with some cutting out of defects, gives almost as good quality as the second grade. Some of the natural features and manufacturing imperfections are not much more numerous in the third grade than in the second grade, but the number and size of the knots are considerably greater, and often the back of the pieces is of lower quality. Where smoothest appearance at close inspection is required under exposure to the weather, first Finish grade gives the best results.

For painted surfaces that do not receive close inspection (barns, summer cotttages, and the like) and where protection against the weather is as important as appearance, the first and second Board grades are satisfactory. The larger knots and pitch pockets in the second grade Common softwood boards do not give as smooth and lasting a painted surface as do the smaller ones in the first grade, but the general utility is good.

TIGHTNESS FACTOR

First grade Common softwood and Utility hardwood boards are suitable for protection against rain or other free water beating or seeping through walls or similar construction. These and the Finish grades are usually kept drier at the lumber yards than are the lower grades, and will therefore shrink and open less at the joints if used without further drying. Where only tightness against leakage of small grain is required in a granary or grain bin, second grade boards may be used with a small amount of cutting to eliminate knotholes. When used as sheathing with good building paper, second grade boards are satisfactory even though knotholes and other similar openings do occur.

WEAR-RESISTANCE FACTOR

Edge-grained material wears better than flat grain, narrow-ringed wears better than wide-ringed, and clear wood wears more evenly than wood containing knots. The first Finish grades in softwoods and hardwoods ordinarily contain very few defects and withstand wear excellently. The second grade in softwoods and in hardwoods sufficiently limits knots and surface characteristics to assure good wearing qualities. Third Finish grade and first grade boards limit the size and character of knots, although not the number, and are satisfactory where maximum uniformity of wear is not required.

DECAY-RESISTANCE FACTOR

Any natural resistance to decay that a wood may have is in the heartwood. The decay resistance of the species so far as affected by grade therefore depends upon the proportion of heartwood in the grade. While this is true of all species, it is of practical importance only in woods with medium or highly decay-resistant heartwood.

The lower grades usually contain more heartwood than do the Select grades. If decay resistance is really needed for the purpose at hand, the first and second board grades are more decay-resistant than are the Finish grades, except in the case of the special Finish grades known as All Heart.

The full decay resistance of grades below the second grade is reduced by the presence of decay that may have existed in the tree or log before it was sawn into lumber. Under conditions conducive to decay, such original decay may spread, although some types of decay, notably peck in cypress, red heart in pine, and white pocket in Douglas-fir, are definitely known to cease functioning once the lumber is properly seasoned.

214

PRICE FACTOR

The spread in price between Select Finish and Utility Board grades varies considerably from time to time, depending upon supply and demand. The cost of the lower Select grades is substantially greater than the upper Board grades of softwoods. With such a difference in price it is obviously important not to buy a better grade than is needed. *Any tendency to buy the best the market offers for all uses is wasteful of both lumber and money*, for in uses such as sheathing, the lower and cheaper grades will render as long and satisfactory service as the higher priced grades.

The price spread between the combined grade of first and second Finish grades and the Common grades of hardwoods is also large. This is of minor importance to builders because most of the hardwood purchased by them has already been manufactured into some form of finished product, such as flooring or interior trim.

Roughly the combined grade of first and second Finish may have a market value from 50 to 100 percent greater than that of the highest Common grade, and contain from 25 to 50 percent more clear-face cuttings of the sizes specified in the grading rules. If large clear-face pieces are required, they can best and possibly only be obtained from the first and second grades. But if only medium-sized or small clear-face pieces are required, they can be obtained from the Common grades.

Appendix II
Standard Lumber Items

Lumber is sold as a number of standard general-purpose items and also as certain special-purpose items. Retail lumberyards carry all the general-purpose items and the more important of the special-purpose items. Some lumber items can be obtained only in the upper grades, and others only in the lower. Few items are made in a complete range of grades. A brief description of framing, dimension, boards, siding, and other lumber and related items commonly carried by most retail lumberyards is given later in this section.

Many lumberyards carry stock items in wood species besides those common to the United States. Larger lumber companies may also have their own sash and door plants and can make to order any wood unit listed in the plans or specifications of frame buildings. The popularity of the wood truss has also brought about the fabrication of these items at many lumberyards.

DRESSED THICKNESSES AND WIDTHS OF LUMBER

Lumber as ordinarily stocked in retail yards is surfaced (dressed) on two sides and two edges. This is to make the lumber ready to use and uniform in size without further reworking, and also to avoid paying transportation costs on material that would have to be cut off on the job. The amount that is reasonable and desirable to dress off has varied considerably in the past and has been the subject of some controversy and misunderstanding among producing and consuming groups. American lumber standards have been set up by the lumber trade with the assistance of Government agencies in such a way as to largely take care of the situation.

American lumber standards and common trade practices now provide dressed sizes as summarized in Table 1 which is taken from the American Softwood Lumber Standard Voluntary Product Standard PS 20-70. The column designated *nominal* shows the dimensions according to which lumber is usually described; the last column shows the actual dimensions of lumber when it is sold surfaced.

When the dimensions of dressed lumber are less than those shown in the table for the actual sizes enumerated, the lumber is known as substandard. Items of some woods are commonly sold in substandard sizes. It is well to check the dimensions before selecting a wood so that allowance can be made in both price and utility for substandard sizes or proper credit given for oversizes.

FRAMING AND DIMENSION

Dimension is primarily framing lumber, such as joists, rafters, and wall studs. It also comprises the planking used for heavy barn floors. Strength, stiffness, and uniformity of size are essential requirements. Framing or Dimension lumber is stocked in all lumberyards but often in only one or two of the general-purpose construction woods—Douglas fir, southern yellow pine, white fir, hemlock, or spruce. It is usually a nominal 2 inches thick, dressed one or two sides to 1 1/2 inches dry (table 2). It is nominally 4, 6, 8, 10, or 12 inches in width, and 8 to 20 feet long in multiples of 2 feet. Dimension lumber thicker than 2 (up to 5) inches and longer than 20 feet is manufactured only in comparatively small quantities.

Perhaps the one most suitable grade for permanent construction wall framing, based on economy and performance, is the third grade in the various species. The grade most generally suitable for joists and rafters for permanent and first-class construction is the second grade of the various species. Satisfactory construction is possible with lower grades, but pieces must be selected and there is considerably more cutting loss. Many species have structural grade classifications permitting use for trusses and other structural components. These structural grades allow greater loads than do equal spans of the lower grades.

Table 1. Nominal and minimum-dressed sizes of boards, dimension, and timbers. (The thicknesses apply to all widths and all widths to all thicknesses.)

ITEM	THICKNESSES			FACE WIDTHS		
	NOMINAL	Minimum Dressed		NOMINAL	Minimum Dressed	
		Dry[6]	Green[6]		Dry[6]	Green[6]
		Inches	*Inches*		*Inches*	*Inches*
Boards[7]				2	1½	1 9/16
				3	2½	2 9/16
				4	3½	3 9/16
				5	4½	4⅝
	1	¾	25/32	6	5½	5⅝
				7	6½	6⅝
	1¼	1	1 1/32	8	7¼	7½
				9	8¼	8½
	1½	1¼	1 9/32	10	9¼	9½
				11	10¼	10½
				12	11¼	11½
				14	13¼	13½
				16	15¼	15½
Dimension				2	1½	1 9/16
				3	2½	2 9/16
				4	3½	3 9/16
	2	1½	1 9/16	5	4½	4⅝

Item	Thickness Nominal	Thickness Min. Dry	Thickness Min. Green	Width Nominal	Width Min. Dry	Width Min. Green
Dimension	2½	2	2 1/16	6	5½	5 5/8
	3	2½	2 9/16	8	7¼	7½
	3½	3	3 1/16	10	9¼	9½
				12	11¼	11½
				14	13¼	13½
				16	15¼	15½
Dimension	4	3½	3 9/16	2	1½	1 9/16
	4½	4	4 1/16	3	2½	2 9/16
				4	3½	3 9/16
				5	4½	4 5/8
				6	5½	5 5/8
				8	7¼	7½
				10	9¼	9½
				12	11¼	11½
				14		13½
				16		15½
Timbers	5 & Thicker		½ Off	5 & Wider		½ Off

⁶ "Dry" lumber has been dried to 19 percent moisture content or less; "green" lumber has a moisture content of more than 19 percent.

⁷ "Boards less than the minimum thickness for 1 inch nominal but ⅝ inch or greater thickness dry (11/16 inch green) may be regarded as American Standard Lumber, but such boards shall be marked to show the size and condition of seasoning at the time of dressing. They shall also be distinguished from 1-inch boards on invoices and certificates.

SHINGLES

Most wooden shingles available in retail lumberyards are of western red cedar, although redwood, white cedar, and cypress are also sometimes stocked. Three grades of shingles are classed under Red Cedar Shingle Bureau rules in three lengths:

No. 1 Blue Label shingles are all clear, all heart, and all edge grain, and are used for the best work as they are less likely to warp.

No. 2 Red Label shingles have clear butts about two-thirds to three-quarters of their length and may contain some flat grain and a little sapwood. This grade is often used for roofs of secondary buildings or to cover sidewalls.

No. 3 Black Label shingles have knots and other defects that are undesirable for surface exposure, but have a 6- to 10-inch clear butt depending on their length. This grade is sometimes used as the undercourse in double-course application of sidewalls. An under-coursing shingle is produced expressly for use on double-course sidewalls.

Shingles are produced in three lengths—16, 18, and 24 inches. The 16-inch shingle, the one most likely to be stocked by retail lumberyards, has a standard thickness designated as 5/2-16 (five shingles measure 2 inches thick at the butt when green). The 16-inch shingles are based on a 5-inch exposure when used on roofs, and four bundles will cover 100 square feet (one square). When used in single-course sidewall application, three bundles of 16-inch shingles will cover 100 square feet laid with a 7-inch exposure. Bundled shingles come in random widths of 3 inches and up. Five 18-inch shingles measure 2 1/4 inches at the butt, and four 24-inch shingles measure 2 inches at the butt when green.

DOOR AND WINDOW FRAMES

Wooden door and window frames, sash, and other similar millwork items are sometimes available in retail lumberyards in standard sizes. Sash and door manufacturers produce ready-hung window units, and the frame, weather-stripped sash and trim are prefitted, assembled, and ready to be placed in the rough wall opening. However, in smaller retail yards it is usually necessary to order before actual use because many window and door sizes and styles are not stock items.

Ponderosa pine is a species used by most manufacturers for frames and window sash, but southern pine and Douglas fir are sometimes used for frame parts. Frames for outside doors are usually provided with oak sills to increase their resistance to wear. However, some sills of the softer woods are supplied with metal edgings located at the wearing surfaces.

Most present-day millwork such as door and window frames, sash, and exterior doors are treated at the factory with a water-repellent preservative. This treatment not only aids in resisting moisture but also in minimizing decay hazards.

STRUCTURAL INSULATING BOARD

Many types of sheet materials in addition to plywood are being used for sheathing walls because they are easily applied and resist racking. Structural insulating board sheathing in 1/2- and 25/32-inch thicknesses is available in 2- by 8-foot and 4- by 8-foot sheets. The 2- by 8-foot sheets are applied horizontally and usually have shallow V or tongued-and-grooved edges. The 4- by 8-foot sheets are square-edged and applied vertically with perimeter nailing. These building boards are made water-resistant by means of an asphalt coating or by impregnation.

When insulating board sheathing is applied with the 2- by 8-foot sheets horizontal, the construction normally is not rigid enough. Auxiliary bracing, such as 1- by 4-inch let-in bracing, is necessary.

A wall with enough rigidity to withstand wind forces can be built with 4- by 8-foot panels of three types—regular-density sheathing 25/32 inch thick, intermediate-density material 1/2 inch thick, or nail-base grades. Panels must be installed vertically and properly nailed. Each manufacturer of insulating board has recommended nailing schedules to satisfy this requirement.

Interior structural insulating board 1/2 inch thick and laminated paperboard in 1/2- and 3/8-inch thickness may be obtained in 4- by 8-foot sheets painted on one side, or in paneled form for use as an interior covering material. These materials are also produced in a tongued-and-grooved ceiling tile in sizes from 12 by 12 inches to 16 by 32 inches; thicknesses vary between 1/2 and 1 inch. They may be designed to serve as a prefinished decorative insulating tile or to provide acoustical qualities. The present practice of manufacturers is to furnish interior board either plain or acoustical with a flamespread-retardant paint finish.

HIGH-DENSITY HARDBOARD

High-density hardboard in standard or tempered form is commonly supplied in 1/8- and 1/4-inch-thick sheets of 4- by 8-foot size. It may be used for both interior and exterior covering material. As with plywood or medium hardboard, the high-density hardboard in the thicker types can be applied vertically with batten strips, or horizontally as a lap siding.

It is often used in the construction of barn doors and for interior lining of barns and other buildings. In perforated form, both types of hardboard are used as soffit material under cornice overhangs to ventilate attic spaces. In untreated form, high-density hardboard of special grade is also used as an underlayment for resilient flooring materials. Hardboards can be obtained with decorative laminated surfaces that provide a pleasing appearance as interior paneling.

PARTICLEBOARD

Particleboard, a sheet material made up of resin-bonded wood particles, is most often used as an underlayment for resilient flooring. It is also adaptable as covering material for interior walls or other uses where they are not exposed to moisture. Particleboard is usually supplied in 4- by 8-foot sheets and in 3/8-inch thickness for paneling, in 5/8-inch thickness for underlayment, and in block form for flooring. It is also used for cabinet and closet doors and as core stock for table tops and other furniture.

Index

Index